It's Not
the End
of the
World

Joan Borysenko

Also by Joan Borysenko, Ph.D.

Books

Minding the Body, Mending the Mind
Guilt Is the Teacher, Love Is the Lesson
On Wings of Light (with Joan Drescher)
Fire in the Soul
Pocketful of Miracles
The Power of the Mind to Heal
(with Miroslav Borysenko, Ph.D.)*
A Woman's Book of Life
*7 Paths to God**
A Woman's Journey to God
*Inner Peace for Busy People**
*Inner Peace for Busy Women**
Saying Yes to Change (with Gordon Dveirin, Ed.D.)*
Your Soul's Compass (with Gordon Dveirin, Ed.D.)*

Audio Programs

*Reflections on a Woman's Book of Life**
A Woman's Spiritual Retreat
Menopause: Initiation into Power
*Minding the Body, Mending the Mind**
*The Beginner's Guide to Meditation**

Video Programs

*Inner Peace for Busy People**
*The Power of the Mind to Heal**

Guided-Meditation CDs

*Meditations for Courage and Compassion**
*Meditations for Relaxation and Stress Reduction**
*Meditations for Self-Healing and Inner Power**
*Invocation of the Angels**

*Available from Hay House

Please visit Hay House USA: **www.hayhouse.com®**
Hay House Australia: **www.hayhouse.com.au**
Hay House UK: **www.hayhouse.co.uk**
Hay House South Africa: **www.hayhouse.co.za**
Hay House India: **www.hayhouse.co.in**

It's Not the End of the World

of the World

Developing Resilience in Times of Change

Joan Borysenko, Ph.D.

HAY HOUSE, INC.
Carlsbad, California • New York City
London • Sydney • Johannesburg
Vancouver • Hong Kong • New Delhi

Published and distributed in the United States by: Hay House, Inc.: www.hayhouse.com • **Published and distributed in Australia by:** Hay House Australia Pty. Ltd.: www.hayhouse.com.au • **Published and distributed in the United Kingdom by:** Hay House UK, Ltd.: www.hayhouse.co.uk • **Published and distributed in the Republic of South Africa by:** Hay House SA (Pty), Ltd.: www.hayhouse.co.za • **Distributed in Canada by:** Raincoast: www.raincoast.com • **Published in India by:** Hay House Publishers India: www.hayhouse.co.in

Editorial supervision: Jill Kramer • *Design:* Riann Bender

Library of Congress Cataloging-in-Publication Data

Borysenko, Joan.
  It's not the end of the world : developing resilience in times of change / Joan Borysenko. -- 1st ed.
       p. cm.
  ISBN 978-1-4019-2632-8 (hbk. : alk. paper) 1. Resilience (Personality trait) 2. Change. I. Title.
  BF698.35.R47B67 2009
  155.2'4--dc22   2009007291

ISBN: 978-1-4019-2632-8

12   11   10   09   6   5   4   3
1st edition, September 2009
3rd edition, November 2009

Printed in the United States of America

For my husband, Gordon F. Dveirin.
I waited so long for you.
And it was worth every second.

CONTENTS

Hope Rules

*"What the caterpillar calls the end of the world,
the master calls a butterfly."*
— Richard Bach

A new world is emerging at warp speed, and some of us will do better than others adapting to it. One laid-off programmer goes home and writes code that turns his iPhone into a xylophone. In ten months he's a millionaire, catapulted into programmer heaven by megasales on Apple's innovative App Store. A second laid-off programmer stresses out and spends his days worried, bored, and depressed.

I've always been fascinated by the differences between these two kinds of people. Their outer circumstances are identical, but they respond to change in radically different ways. One gives up and the other takes off. One clings to the past, while the other becomes the future.

> UNDERSTANDING THAT THE FUTURE ISN'T
> SOMETHING THAT HAPPENS TO YOU, BUT
> SOMETHING THAT *YOU* CREATE IS THE KEY
> TO SURVIVING AND THRIVING IN CHANGING
> TIMES. THAT'S WHAT THIS BOOK IS ALL ABOUT.

We can all recite the fearful story line of the 21st century: The global climate is changing for the worse. A mass die-off of species is under way. Terrorists breed panic and uncertainty. Financial worry creates chronic stress and threatens the survival of business as usual here and abroad. The world population resembles a bacterial culture that has outgrown its petri dish. Pandemics crouch in the wings, ready to pounce. And that's just the beginning of the familiar litany.

But what if there's a more hopeful way to understand this postmodern story—this parenthesis between what used to be and the innovative, sustainable future that can be? Those who will thrive and create that new future are the ones with enough vision and resilience to see the hope through the hype.

The late physicist Ilya Prigogine, who completed his distinguished career at the University of Texas at Austin, which now houses his Center for Complex Quantum Systems, won a Nobel Prize in 1977 for his theory of dissipative structures. Simply put, all complex systems from subatomic particles to human civilizations reach a point where their current level of organization becomes unstable. Then they melt down. When the old system crashes, it can then reconfigure in a better way, free from the determinism of the past. Prigogine called this daunting event an "escape to a higher order." That's where we are at this moment in history, and although the changes we face are disconcerting in the short run, they're a prelude to great possibility.

The Chinese character for change is made up of two characters: danger and opportunity. The *danger* lies in giving in to the fear that accompanies the loss of the familiar. Fear is poisonous to creativity because when we're in survival mode, the tendency is to regress and hole up in some "safe haven," often turning to alcohol, drugs, television, or rigid ideologies.

The *opportunity* of change, on the other hand, lies in being ejected from our comfort zone. Like a cave dweller suddenly thrust into the light, it takes a while to adjust. But when we open our eyes and look around with an open mind and a curious heart, a whole new world of possibilities reveals itself.

My purpose in writing this book is to help you overcome fear; stress less; and learn how resilient, creative people think and act. At the risk of sounding prophetic, I believe that in a few years, a new kind of natural selection will have its way with humanity. Hopeful, stress-hardy people will rule the world. And as change and uncertainty escalate, which is likely, those who are stress prone will be less and less able to compete. Read on, and take your place in the new world that's emerging.

INTRODUCTION

Getting from Stress to Strength

"We are all in the gutter,
but some of us are looking at the stars."
— Oscar Wilde

Shortly after the economy crashed in the fall of 2008, I was slated to give a lecture on converting stress to strength at a conference of about a thousand people. I'm reasonably stress hardy, but I'm not immune to a good shake-up when circumstances call for it. Losing nearly a third of my hard-won retirement in the stock market—and not knowing whether to let the remainder ride or to bury it in the backyard—had me on edge . . . although that's a good place to be when you're an observer of human nature.

How were other people responding to being out of control financially? I wondered. A stunning example of two different coping styles emerged at the conference.

Picture this: It's a warm North Carolina evening when I arrive, and several of the speakers are gathered for dinner. Some of them are moderately famous and very well-heeled. "We could use your help on Wall Street," a renowned financial adviser tells me between bites of fish. "I know a guy who just lost everything and killed himself . . . actually jumped out a window."

An awkward silence settles over the room where we're dining, relieved only by the sounds of frogs and crickets filtering in from the moonlit field outside. I think what a pity it is that a young man—a son, a husband, a father—would choose to give up and die rather than try to re-create his life. The financial guru looks over to me and says, "My whole Rolodex could use your services." Then he smiles and turns pensive. "Just remember. Everything in the world is a duality. When one thing goes down, something else goes up. Right now the economy is in the toilet, and stress management is on the upswing."

"So are psychics," I reply. "At this point, they know more than economists."

We all laugh nervously and go back to eating our dinners. In a few minutes, people begin to filter out, and I go searching for a cup of tea. "Devon," one of the other speakers (her topic was business planning), grabs a cup of coffee and we stand around together, passing the time of day companionably. She tells me a riveting story.

Less than a year before, Devon and her husband had owned a successful mortgage-brokerage firm and real-estate agency. But when the housing market bit the dust, so did their companies. In just a few months, they were broke and more than a half-million dollars in debt. Their luxurious home was gone, as were most of the material perks of wealth they'd enjoyed.

Their family, which included three young daughters, relocated to a modest apartment. Within a few months, Devon and her husband started a new business developing and marketing a product that helps prevent elderly people from falling, which is a major cause of disability and death. While it will take time for the business to grow, Devon seems relaxed and confident.

"You know, I haven't felt so close to my family in years. While things are tough money-wise, we've all come together in a really great way. I'm working at home now and seeing much more of the girls," she tells me. "Life is short, and I understand close-up and personal that material things come and go. Everything has its day. It may sound trite, but I really get that loving one another is the most important thing. So in a weird kind of way, I'm grateful for the big changes we're going through. I'm a different person now—a little wiser and a whole lot happier."

Who would *you* rather be? The Wall Street broker who despaired and jumped out of the window or Devon, who was already creating a future she liked better than her financially successful past. Even though her new business was a gamble, she was already happy, unwilling to bet the emotional farm on what might or might not happen later.

The difference between Devon and the stockbroker hit close to home for me. My father, who was a perpetually stressed and worried man, jumped out of a window more than 30 years ago rather than live with cancer. As a result of his sudden death, I left a stable and promising career as a cancer cell biologist and assistant professor of anatomy and cell biology at the Tufts University School of Medicine in Boston.

Many of my colleagues thought I'd lost my mind to walk away from a career that I'd spent seven years of graduate and postgraduate work training for, especially when I was just about to go up for tenure and promotion, which seemed like a sure bet. But I underwent a *metanoia*—a change of heart that altered the course of my life. While I knew a lot about cancer *cells,* it was clear that I knew almost nothing about *people* with cancer. My hope was that if I could help other stressed people become more resilient, it would give a positive meaning to my father's death. That became my guiding vision and heartfelt mission.

Through a fortunate set of synchronicities, I was able to retrain in a new field called behavioral medicine and cofound a mind-body clinic at one of the Harvard Medical School teaching hospitals with my colleague and mentor Herbert Benson, M.D. Dr. Benson is known for his discovery of the *relaxation response,* the body's innate antidote to the stress response. In a short time, I was running a clinic for people with stress-related disorders, chronic illnesses, AIDS, and cancer. Since leaving the clinic in 1988,

I've worked with people from all walks of life, coping with every kind of challenge. These many years of experience with individuals, corporations, and hospitals have deepened my insights about how to live our best lives—a process that's brought into sharp focus by sudden change. Sharing the "secrets" I've learned along the way is my passion. It's also my father's last gift to us all.

Here's how this book is organized: Part I, "Why Smart Cookies Don't Crumble," comprises four chapters that provide the foundation you need in order to become flexible and adaptive in the face of change. You'll learn what 30 years of research has revealed about the differences between people like Devon and the ill-fated stockbroker. This will give you the framework so you can get down to business in a practical way and learn to think and act like a resilient, highly creative person. Part II of the book, "Train Your Brain for Success," provides the necessary tools for developing new neural pathways that can transform your thinking and your life. Part III, "Become the Future," guides you in defining your values and discovering your ultimate vision and purpose.

I wrote this book to teach you how to hold fear in the palm of your hand without being burned by its fire. I know that you can do it. Whatever may be going on for you, remember . . . it's not the end of the world. It's a call to the genius that lies asleep within you—and within all of us—a genius that is ready and able to re-create the world.

Why Smart Cookies Don't Crumble[1]

CHAPTER ONE

The Three Secrets of Resilience

"Get a lot of sleep, a lot of exercise. Eat real good.
Say your prayers. And be good to your dogs."
— Mickey Rourke

(His response to the question, "What is your advice to survive
and come back in hard times?"[1])

I was sitting in a CNN greenroom in front of a plate of stale bagels. A *greenroom,* in case you've never been in one, isn't green at all—it's just an ordinary waiting room populated by nervous people waiting to be guests on radio or TV shows. My first book, *Minding the Body, Mending the Mind,* had earned me an interview on *Sonya Live,* an intelligent and lively talk show hosted by psychologist Sonya Friedman. Sitting right next to the bagels was her most recent book, *Smart Cookies Don't Crumble.* I tried to take the witty title to heart, but the sound of the blood pounding in my ears was a distraction.

Let's not crumble here, Joan, I thought. *This interview isn't a disaster in the making—it's an opportunity to get your message out!* Somehow I picked my way onto the set, circumnavigating the maze of snaking wires that don't show up on your TV screen. Wiping beads of cold sweat from my face, I took a seat across from Sonya. She was composed, poised, and interested in the topic of mind-body medicine. And, of course, she was a pro who'd been sitting in the catbird seat for years. I, on the other hand, was a rank amateur in a completely new situation . . . one with the potential to humiliate me from coast to coast. Worse still, my mother was watching.

Although I was in a mild state of terror at the beginning of the interview, by the end I'd managed to relax and come back home to myself. I not only survived—I even managed to have a little fun. This bouncing back from stress is called *resilience.* It's a graceful way of flowing through life, adapting to different circumstances with the ease of water assuming the shape of whatever container it's poured into. Resilience is also a courageous affirmation of life in the face of more serious stresses such as illness, divorce, job loss, financial setback, abuse, war, and terror.

Stress and Resilience

Let's take a closer look at how stress and resilience work. Think of a rubber band: When it's stretched out, there's stress on the rubber, but when you release that stress, it snaps back into shape. That's the most basic kind of resilience. But if the rubber band is stretched for a long time, it eventually begins to fatigue and is more likely to *give out.*

The same is true for the human body and mind: we tend to give out when we're stressed for long periods. Studies estimate that 75 to 90 percent of visits to the family doctor are for conditions caused or made worse by stress. These include headaches, digestive disturbances, infertility, memory loss, heart problems, allergies, high blood pressure, immune disorders, blood-sugar control for diabetics, back pain, fatigue, anxiety, depression, and many other illnesses.

When an emergency calls for sudden "stretching," most healthy people can rise to the challenge. Imagine that you've just tripped over the cord to your laptop and it goes flying off the table. Without having to think about it, your body releases adrenaline and you suddenly have the agility of an outfielder for the Boston Red Sox. With a little luck, you can even catch that laptop! Your sudden athletic prowess is due to an automatic overdrive system called the *fight-or-flight response* that kicks in for survival purposes. When the emergency is over, your "rubber band" relaxes, and you return to a resting state of balance and ease.

But what if the stressor doesn't go away? After all, life is much more complex than flying laptops with short trajectories. The fight-or-flight system evolved before chronic stresses like those of a company seeking a bailout in a struggling economy, families juggling mounting credit-card debt, or losing your pension just as you're ready to retire. If you can't release tension, then stress becomes chronic and you become more prone to illness, depression, anger, and anxiety. And instead of enjoying life as the creative adventure that resilient people perceive it to be, you get side-lined and stuck.

One of the most famous scales for evaluating stress levels and correlating them with illness was designed in 1967 by two psychiatrists, Thomas Holmes and Richard Rahe. Their scale measures stress in Life Change Units (LCUs). For example, the most stressful change, the death of a spouse, rates 100 LCUs. Getting married rates a 50. After all, learning to pick up your dirty socks (or living with someone who doesn't), agreeing on a budget, or discovering that your beloved snores can all be stressful life changes. Taking out a small loan or mortgage was worth 17 LCUs in the mid-1960s. These days, however, when job loss and foreclosures are so high, it might garner even more points.

Holmes and Rahe gave the test to thousands of people and correlated their scores with health.[2] The higher the score, the more likely their subjects were to get sick. A score of more than 300 LCUs is associated with a high risk of illness, while scores between 150 and 300 correlate with a moderate risk of illness. You can find a copy of the Holmes and Rahe stress scale for adults and youth on Wikipedia (**http://en.wikipedia .org/wiki/Holmes_and_Rahe_stress_scale**). The scale has been tested in both men and women, as well as in different cultures. Holmes's and Rahe's pioneering research helped define the role of change in stress and set the scene for understanding resilience.

What's My Number?

You can get a simple read on your stress level by placing your finger on the measurement line on the following page, corresponding to how stressed or relaxed you feel right now. Are you a 20, a 30, or perhaps a 75?

Repeat the reading each day at the same time (do so before meals, since eating is usually a relaxing activity), and record your measurements for a month on the chart. Is your daily number decreasing as you practice the exercises in the book? If not, consider getting professional help.

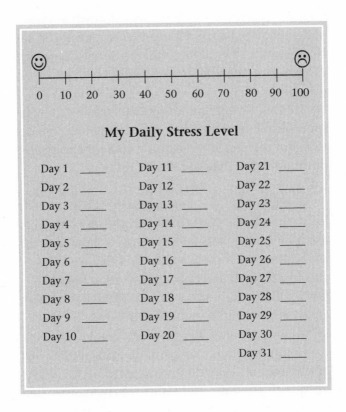

My Daily Stress Level

Day 1 ____	Day 11 ____	Day 21 ____
Day 2 ____	Day 12 ____	Day 22 ____
Day 3 ____	Day 13 ____	Day 23 ____
Day 4 ____	Day 14 ____	Day 24 ____
Day 5 ____	Day 15 ____	Day 25 ____
Day 6 ____	Day 16 ____	Day 26 ____
Day 7 ____	Day 17 ____	Day 27 ____
Day 8 ____	Day 18 ____	Day 28 ____
Day 9 ____	Day 19 ____	Day 29 ____
Day 10 ____	Day 20 ____	Day 30 ____
		Day 31 ____

The Three Secrets of Resilience

Ironically, the serious trauma that soldiers experience in battle has recently become a living laboratory for resilience. Dr. Steven Southwick, himself a veteran of the Vietnam War, is deputy director of the Clinical Neurosciences Division of the National Center for PTSD (post-traumatic stress disorder).

He said, "We do know there are factors that make some people resilient. There are genetic components to it, but there's a huge learning component. People can train themselves to be more resilient."[3]

Resilience, as you might expect, is big business for corporations. Numerous consulting companies teach businesses and their employees how to stress less and become more adaptable and creative in trying circumstances. Diane Coutu, a writer for the *Harvard Business Review,* summarized much of what they teach in an excellent article published in 2002.[4]

Coutu analyzed research data from studies that investigated resilience in diverse populations, including at-risk children, Holocaust survivors, prisoners of war, businesses and their employees, people with life-challenging illnesses, and survivors of abuse. She also interviewed some fascinating people who'd lived through unsettling times and had come out better for the challenge.

She interviewed Dean Becker, the president and CEO of a company called Adaptiv Learning Systems that teaches resilience. Becker said, "More than education, more than experience, more than training, a person's level of resilience will determine who succeeds and who fails. That's true in the cancer ward, it's true in the Olympics, and it's true in the boardroom."[5]

Coutu identified three traits of resilient thinking. As you read through them in the remainder of this chapter, consider these secrets a map for healthy thinking that can reduce your stress and help you discover your best future.

"Resilience is a reflex, a way of facing and understanding the world, that is deeply etched into a person's mind and soul. Resilient people and companies face reality with staunchness, make meaning of hardship instead of crying out in despair, and improvise solutions from thin air. Others do not."
— Diane Coutu

Secret #1:
A Resolute Acceptance of Reality

So there I was ready to go on *Sonya Live* and scared witless. It occurred to me that greenrooms might not be named for the color of their walls, but for the color of their occupants. What to do in the face of this stressor? I suppose I could have hidden in the bathroom, but that would have been unseemly. It would have also killed off my fledgling media career. The simple fact was that I was a scheduled guest on a popular television show. I needed to rise to the occasion, whatever it took.

RESILIENT THINKERS FACE DIFFICULT SITUA-
TIONS HEAD-ON. THEN THEY DO WHATEVER
IT TAKES TO SURVIVE. HOW ABOUT YOU? DO
YOU ACCEPT YOUR SITUATION REALISTICALLY;
OR ARE YOU MORE PRONE TO DENIAL, RATIO-
NALIZATION, OR WISHFUL THINKING?

Resilient thinkers face difficult situations head-on. Then they do whatever it takes to survive. For example, if you own a restaurant-supply business but people aren't eating out, you're in trouble. If you're a construction worker and no new buildings are going up, the writing is on the wall. The faster you're able to see the truth and take a good hard look at how you can modify your business to adjust to the situation, the better you'll do.

Getting hired at McDonald's or bagging groceries at the supermarket may not be your idea of career heaven, but it still brings in some cash that could make the difference between staying in your home and losing it. Taking jobs like these when there's no other choice at hand shows the resolute acceptance of reality that characterizes the resilient mind-set.

Rationalization ("Lots of people are behind on their mortgage, but the government will get us out of this soon"), denial ("Things aren't so bad; I'm bound to get some orders soon"), and wishful thinking ("I'll just visualize myself living in a mansion and say some affirmations") are common coping strategies when things get tough. But burying your head in the sand won't put dinner on the table. You can only get through chaotic times if you have a clear, realistic picture of what's actually taking place. This is true both for businesses and for each of us personally.

Perhaps you've just been diagnosed with a serious illness. While it always pays to have hope, resilience requires you to look your diagnosis straight in the eye and make appropriate plans for treatment, manage financial responsibilities, update your will, and get the necessary support at every level. In other words, given the reality of whatever your situation is, what's needed to manage it?

> IT'S TIME TO BITE THE BULLET. FACING REAL-ITY CAN BE EMOTIONALLY TRYING IN THE SHORT RUN, BUT LIFESAVING LATER ON. SIT DOWN WITH A TRUSTED FRIEND AND TELL HIM OR HER WHAT THE REALITY OF YOUR SITUATION IS, AS BEST AS YOU KNOW IT.

Diane Coutu told the following story in her article "How Resilience Works." When the World Trade Center was bombed in 1993, financial giant Morgan Stanley faced the reality that the highly symbolic building they occupied was a prime terror-ist target. The company responded by implement-ing escape drills, which they expected everyone to attend and take seriously. They also designated three safe locations elsewhere for employees to congregate where they could continue their business activities in case of disaster.

This heads-up attitude proved lifesaving eight years later on 9/11 when two hijacked airplanes destroyed the iconic twin towers and killed nearly 3,000 people. Luck was also on Morgan Stanley's side since their 2,700 employees were all in the south tower, which was the second to be struck. The first tower was hit at 8:46 A.M. By 8:47, the company's employees were starting to evacuate. Fifteen minutes later, the second plane crashed into the south tower, but by that time, the offices of Morgan Stanley were almost empty. In spite of receiving an almost direct hit, only seven employees were lost, including the vice president of security, Rick Rescorla, who had designed the escape drills and stayed behind with a bullhorn, keeping the employees calm and ushering them to safety. Rescorla was himself a resilient, highly decorated Vietnam vet who'd learned to put other people's needs ahead of his own.

Secret #2:
A Deep Belief That Life Is Meaningful

Two weeks after 9/11, I facilitated a spiritual retreat just outside of New York City. It was an intensely emotional time for the whole country, but especially for two young Manhattan roommates who were attending the retreat together. Their balcony faced the World Trade Center, and they'd witnessed the twin towers falling firsthand. Both of them were having flashbacks and nightmares—signs of PTSD—and trying to make sense of the shock and terror.

One of the young men had already turned to the work of Viktor Frankl, a resilient Austrian psychiatrist who survived four Nazi death camps and then wrote the classic book *Man's Search for Meaning.* Frankl was inspired by the statement of philosopher Friedrich Nietzsche: "That which does not kill me makes me stronger." In spite of the unthinkable trauma and hardship he suffered during the Holocaust, Frankl became a happy man and an inspiration to millions of people worldwide. The key to resilience, he believed, was to find positive meaning in traumatic experience.

When tempted to give up hope in the death camps, he found a reason to live by setting his sights on giving seminars on resilience to people after the war. He was determined to make positive use of the hard lessons he was learning.

How would your life be different if this was the attitude with which you approached even the worst imaginable circumstances?

———————◆———————

"Those who have a 'why' to live for can bear with almost any 'how.'"
— **Friedrich Nietzsche**

———————◆———————

The most deeply held values that give meaning to our lives are often spiritual in nature. Feeling an authentic connection to a larger intelligence, whether we relate to it as a loving, forgiving God or a universal energy of compassion, encourages what's best in us. When times get tough, the tough often pray—whether they're in prison camps, at the bedside of loved ones, or in the unemployment line. Faith is highly correlated with resilience, providing a true north that orients us when we're lost in a sea of change or desperation . . . but the face of faith itself is changing.

According to a 2008 poll conducted by the Pew Forum on Religion & Public Life, 92 percent of Americans believe in God or some universal spirit, but the great majority (some 70 percent) believe that there are many paths to God. Other polls indicate that about a third of Americans consider themselves "spiritual eclectics," finding inspiration in various traditions without subscribing to any particular one.

Being spiritual but not religious is a growing trend. Psychiatrist George Vaillant, director of the Study of Adult Development at Harvard Medical School in Boston, and one of the world's leading experts on resilience, points out that many of the best-selling books in America over the past five years have been based either on the spiritual search or "the rejection of the religious in a secular world."[6]

The importance of finding a source of strength and guidance within, and nurturing it through practices such as meditation, applies to everyone—the person of deep religious conviction, the agnostic, and the atheist alike. When the mind calms down, it's easier to relate to the world around us—seeing the beauty in a flower or appreciating the nuances of a smile. These deep connections are sacred and invite positive emotions including awe, joy, gratitude, and compassion that banish stress and cultivate inner strength. Vaillant writes: "Spirituality is not about ideas, sacred texts and theology; rather, spirituality is all about emotions and social connection. Specific religions, for all their limitations, are often the portal through which positive emotions are brought into conscious attention."[7]

Secret #3:
An Uncanny Ability to Improvise

Resilient people are masters of innovation. Their fertile imaginations are expansive, and they attend to details that others might miss or consider irrelevant, using everything at their disposal to create the best possible outcome. Like a child who can transform a kitchen pot into a drum, hat, boat, or scoop for sand, resilient people use their imaginations to improvise solutions with whatever they can find.

The term for making do with whatever is at hand is the French word *bricolage*. One of my clients, whom I'll call Tasha, is a true *bricoleuse*. She recently lost her job as a draftsman at an architectural firm, but true to her resilient nature, Tasha showed up the very next morning at a temporary labor pool and was relieved to make $10 an hour doing whatever work was available. In the course of a month, she temped as a receptionist, filed records in a doctor's office, and watered indoor plants for a landscaping company.

The landscaping job intrigued her even though she had very little responsibility at first. She was hired to schlep water and soak plants, but in just a few weeks, Tasha was offering suggestions for where to move plants for better growth and more aesthetic harmony. She created new indoor landscapes out of existing materials in a way that was both practical and beautiful. The spatial intelligence that served her well as a draftsman helped her segue smoothly into a new career. Within three months, Tasha had been hired full-time by the company and was training to become an interior landscape designer.

To improvise is to create something new that arises organically out of

AVAILABLE RESOURCES. LOOK AROUND THE ROOM YOU'RE IN WITH ALL THE CURIOSITY YOU CAN MUSTER. WHAT COULD BE MOVED TO A DIFFERENT SPOT OR SHIFTED A BIT IN ORDER TO CREATE MORE EFFICIENCY, COMFORT, AND BEAUTY? COULD SOMETHING IN ANOTHER ROOM BE BETTER USED IN THIS ONE?

Improvisation requires attentiveness and mindfulness, which is the ability to see your environment with unabashed curiosity. Concentration-camp inmates who collected bits of string and wire wherever they found them were often the ones who survived. Fashioning a shoelace out of odds and ends could make the difference between freezing to death and living to see another day.

Living in poverty as a graduate student helped cultivate my own ability to improvise. That's why challenge is a good thing. It's an invitation to master new skills that aren't needed in more comfortable circumstances. I supported my young son and student husband on a meager government stipend. When something broke, I had to fix it, as my husband wasn't handy and there was no spare cash to call the Maytag Man. Armed with a screwdriver, a few wrenches, a hammer, some wire, and the greatest invention of the civilized world—duct tape—I could have given Rube Goldberg a run for his money.

Many organizations, of course, hope to recruit people with this talent. During World War II, the American government was recruiting intelligence operatives. Interviewees were asked to describe the waiting room. Those who were skilled at mindfulness, and therefore attentive to their environment, could describe it in phenomenal detail. They could remember things like the placement of doors and windows, the subject matter of pictures, and the color and type of furniture. Since every bit of information comes in handy when a situation calls for a creative response, the most attentive ones were those who got the jobs.

In this chapter, we've explored the three secrets of resilience: an eyes-open acceptance of reality, a deep belief that life is meaningful, and a penchant for creative improvisation. When I first looked at the research on resilience, I was puzzled by the omission of one attitude, which, at first blush, might look critical to resilience.

What is it? You might be surprised that it's *optimism*—that is, the pie-in-the-sky kind that Princeton professor Cornel West calls "cheap optimism." The next chapter will explain how to be an *optimistic realist* and how to recognize and root out both the wishful and pessimistic thinking that can paralyze right action.

CHAPTER TWO

Optimistic Realism

"The pessimist complains about the wind; the optimist expects it to change; the realist adjusts the sails."
— **William Arthur Ward**

Jim Collins, who wrote the book *Good to Great,* assumed that resilient companies were made up of optimistic people. As it turned out, he was dead wrong. When he spoke to Admiral Jim Stockdale, a POW who had been held captive by the Vietcong and tortured for eight years, Collins realized his error. Part of their revealing conversation was reported by Diane Coutu in the *Harvard Business Review:*

> I [Collins] asked Stockdale: "Who didn't make it out of the camps?" And he said, "Oh, that's easy. It was the optimists. They were the ones who said we were going to be out by Christmas. And then

they said we'd be out by Easter and then out by Fourth of July and out by Thanksgiving, and then it was Christmas again." Then Stockdale turned to me and said, "You know, I think they all died of broken hearts."[1]

Studies on former POWs confirm that facing reality is, in fact, one of the keys to resilience. Dr. Steven Southwick, deputy director of the Clinical Neurosciences Division of the National Center for PTSD (post-traumatic stress disorder), is one of the leading experts on resilience exhibited by prisoners of war. He coined the term *realistic optimism* from his observations that resilient people "have a habitual way of explaining events to themselves. They see the negative but don't dwell on it or over-generalize."[2] I call this explanatory style *optimistic realism*—the ability to size up your situation dispassionately, while still staying open to positive future possibilities.

How do *you* explain tough circumstances to yourself? In this chapter, you'll learn how to dissect your thinking style and develop a stress-hardy, realistic way of approaching hard times that has the power to help you create an optimal future.

Your Explanatory Style

Psychologist Martin E. P. Seligman is the founding father of positive psychology. For most of its history, clinical psychology has focused on the negative—dealing with problems like anxiety, depression, anger management, stress, and trauma—but *positive* emotions are a recent field of psychological study. Negative emotions are all about survival and tend to be self-centered and self-defeating. For example, when you're tense and worried, you've probably noticed that it's hard to appreciate what's good about life. Positive emotions such as joy and gratitude, on the other hand, are expansive and welcoming. Life outside of the "gloom cloud" is also more forgiving, grateful, and loving.

Learning to generate positive emotions is an important life skill to which Seligman has devoted considerable research. One of his great contributions is a precise, operational description of how optimists and pessimists think—particularly how they explain negative or stressful events.

This is important information to digest, since we can't change our thinking style until we're aware of it. In my experience, a lot of pessimists believe that they're optimists because of two factors: First, it's more socially acceptable to be an optimist, and people want to be liked so they cast themselves in the best light. Second, most of us weren't taught how to analyze our thinking style, so we don't recognize it for what it really is.

Seligman spent decades studying what's called *explanatory style*. Think of it in this way: What do you say to yourself when something bad happens? How do you explain it? Take a minute and think back to the last time something negative or stressful happened. Did you have a fender bender? An argument with a loved one? Problems at work? Maybe you're having a hard time finding a job or paying your bills. Think about the situation, and write down the thoughts you had about why it happened.

Why Did This Bad Thing Happen?

Take a few minutes right now before you read on. Recall the last time something negative or stressful happened, such as a disagreement with someone, a lost business opportunity, an illness, an overdue bill, and so forth. Don't cheat. *Put this book down and think of an example.* We'll examine it together shortly.

Did you do your homework? Keep it handy. By the time you've finished reading this chapter, you'll know whether you're a pessimist or a stress-hardy, optimistic realist. We'll begin our self-sleuthing exercise by dissecting a suitable example from my own life. Hopefully, it will give you the courage to look fearlessly at your own explanatory style.

True Confessions

I'm a pessimist—albeit a recovering one. That's an excellent credential for teaching people how to change their explanatory styles because I've had to learn from scratch. Optimism doesn't come naturally, so I'm able to break down the skills others need in a way that a more innately upbeat person couldn't begin to fathom.

> WITHOUT AWARENESS OF YOUR THINKING STYLE, IT'S IMPOSSIBLE TO MAKE BETTER DE-CISIONS. *AWARENESS AND CHOICE ARE THE BUILDING BLOCKS OF ADAPTING CREATIVELY TO CHANGE.*

In the next paragraph, you'll read my personal-thought sample, which reveals a classically pessimistic explanatory style. Here's the background: The stock market crashed in the fall of 2008. During those weeks when it kept spiraling downward (and everyone wondered day by day, *When will it hit bottom? Should I hold on? Should I bail out? Is the entire world economy going to implode?*) what did *I* say to myself? My internal dialogue follows. It could be a script for a Woody Allen film.

My Thought Sample

You idiot. You knew that things were going to pieces. You could feel it in your bones and kept thinking about getting out of the market, but did you do it? Oh, no. You had to listen to the experts. "Hold on," they all said. "If you sell on the way down, you can never recoup your losses when the market goes back up again." Fat lot of good that sorry advice did! Now you'll never be able to retire. What if you get sick and can't work anymore? What if no one wants to hire you to give workshops because people don't have the money to come? You try to do everything right, yet you still end up scrambling—it's just not fair.

Dammit! I already work so hard. I have no life and can't see the kids and grandkids nearly as much as I'd like. I can't even get outside and walk the dogs because I'm so busy. Face it, Joan, this is the end.

Not a very enlivening, creative conversation with myself, was it? It's hard enough to experience a stressor, but adding insult to injury with a pessimistic explanatory style is like a one-two punch. Just as you're ready to get up, you knock yourself down again.

Now that you've sampled my explanatory style, we can dissect the three classic pessimistic thought processes that Seligman describes. These three thinking patterns all begin with the letter *P,* which is very handy. It makes your habitual thinking obvious, so it's easier to catch yourself and change your tune. The three *P*'s are *personal, pervasive,* and *permanent.*

The Three Poisons of Pessimistic Thinking

Poison #1: Taking Things Personally

Pessimists take negative events *personally* and blame themselves for their problems. Can you see how I did that in my thought sample? Even the world's smartest financial experts didn't see the impending crash, yet I expected myself to make the right decision about my investments. I called myself an idiot and believed it.

Taking things personally leads to guilt and shame, which are disempowering emotions. Taking

AND IT'S THE STORY OF MY LIFE."
WHAT'S *YOUR* HABITUAL STORY
ABOUT WHY BAD THINGS HAPPEN?

Disputing Your Negative Thoughts

One of the keys to optimistic realism is becoming aware of, and then disputing, your conditioned negative statements. In the lingo of modern psychology, these habitual negative thought processes are called *cognitive distortions*—faulty thinking not based on reality. In the example I gave you from my own life, it's easy to dispute my negative statements. I *do* get out and walk, and I *do* visit my kids and grandkids. My business is doing well, and I'm creative and juiced about life. Furthermore, I'm a reasonably well-adjusted, resilient, successful person. I make mistakes but think of them as learning opportunities. And if you asked people who know me to list my traits, "idiot" is unlikely to be in the top ten.

A good disputation isn't wishful thinking—it's reality. I didn't say that I was a financial mogul, the next Oprah, an Olympic sprinter, or Grandmother of the Year. However, I did make objectively true statements that other people would readily agree with.

If you keep terrorizing yourself with thoughts such as *The economy sucks and there are no jobs out there,* you can dispute your pessimism by thinking of even one other person who has recently found work. It's not cheap optimism to tell yourself that although there are fewer jobs available, all you need is *one.* When you learn how to think like a stress-hardy person, you can escape the prison of your own erroneous, self-centered, negative beliefs and get on board with creating a more positive future.

Stress-Hardy Thinking

Back in 1981, Illinois Bell Telephone (IBT) initiated a major downsizing.[3] They reduced their workforce from 26,000 employees to about half that number in a single year. Today's news is full of similar situations. As you might imagine, the people who lost their jobs at IBT weren't the only ones who were challenged to adjust. Those who stayed on had new roles and responsibilities, and often new bosses. Fortunately, researchers from the University of Chicago had begun a study of about 450 supervisors, managers, and executives at IBT six years before the downsizing. They continued their research until 1987, six years after the restructuring was complete, which gave them a chance to observe how people responded to the changes in the long run.

Lead psychologist Salvatore Maddi and his colleagues found that following the downsizing, about two-thirds of their study group became stressed and showed declines in leadership skills. Many also developed health problems, including obesity, heart attacks, strokes, substance abuse, and depression. That's the bad news.

The good news is that a third of the group thrived even though they went through the same amount of uncertainty that the deregulation and divestiture of IBT had imposed on their colleagues. They remained happy, healthy, and committed to their jobs. (Dr. Maddi is currently a professor at the University of California at Irvine and the founder and director of The Hardiness Institute, also located in Irvine. You can access hardiness trainings online or take a test to assess your degree of hardiness at: **www.hardiness institute.com.**)

The difference between the two groups revolved around three key beliefs that the stress-hardy employees of IBT subscribed to. These beliefs are easy to remember because they each begin with the letter *C:* commitment, control, and challenge.

Commitment

Commitment is about maintaining an ongoing engagement with a potentially stressful situation. It's the opposite of alienation—sticking your head in the sand and mentally checking out. A friend of mine, whom I'll call "Roger," worked in the department of cardiology at a large teaching hospital. The fair and competent physician who was the department chief left and was replaced by the kind of guy who expresses anxiety by criticizing others.

Several staff members became stressed out and complained to one another about this "boss from hell." A few even contemplated looking for new jobs. Roger, however, set up a meeting and asked his new boss what his hopes for the department were, what he (Roger) could do to help realize them, and how the staff might be invited into a dialogue about making the department a model of best practices and compassionate care. That one meeting reduced the new chief's anxiety and sowed the seeds of creative partnership. It was also an expression of Roger's deep commitment to patient-centered medicine and caring for others.

When your work or lifestyle is deeply meaningful and you know what you stand for and what your values are all about, it's easier to deal with stress because you have a higher vision. If difficulties arise at work, the stress-hardy response is to talk to those involved rather than to avoid contact. If there's an important project and you have the skills to do it, volunteer. If there's conflict, try to resolve it. Instead of turning off, tune in. The same skills apply to your personal relationships. If a job or relationship really matters to you, it's worth staying with it and committing yourself to making it better.

Control

Control is the opposite of powerlessness, but it doesn't mean becoming a control freak and trying to bend other people and situations to your will. It means *agency*—that I-can-do-it feeling, which leads to effective action.

In Roger's case, the right action was meaningful dialogue with his new boss. Rather than waiting around passively to see what would happen, Roger opted to find out more about his boss's vision. If you're a parent whose kid is addicted to drugs or computers, control might mean gathering information, getting the support you need, and then taking the necessary but unpleasant step of putting your child in a treatment program. If you find out that you have diabetes, control means learning about the disease, finding the best doctor, eating right, exercising, and taking any prescribed medications—rather than ignoring your health. If you're having marital problems, then talking to your spouse and perhaps finding a good therapist will put you back in control. Ignoring the situation can put you out the door.

Challenge

When Roger was in medical school, his father lost his job and could no longer contribute to his son's hefty tuition. *Instead of interpreting this turn of events as a threat to his dreams, Roger thought of it as a challenge to his ingenuity.* How could he pay the tuition and finish medical school? In a matter of weeks, he'd arranged a student loan and found part-time work in a laboratory. The belief that change is a challenge rather than a threat is an invitation to the improvisational skill of *bricolage,* the creative mind-set central to resilience.

> HOW DO YOU RELATE TO CHANGE? IS IT A THREAT TO THE STATUS QUO OR A CHALLENGE TO GROW AND DEVELOP? PEOPLE WHO THINK OF CHANGE AS A CHALLENGE EXPAND THEIR HORIZONS AND MATURE AS HUMAN BEINGS. THEY'RE ALIVE AND JUICY. ARE YOU?

In the following chapters, you'll learn more about positive psychology and how to optimize your thinking, move on from disappointment or stress, and create your best future.

✦ ✦ ✦

CHAPTER THREE

Helper's High

*"Giving is as good for the giver as it is for the receiver.
Science says it's so. We'll be happier, healthier, and
even—odds are—live a little longer if we're generous."*
— **Dr. Stephen G. Post**

US Airways flight 1549 took off from New York's LaGuardia Airport on January 15, 2009, but less than two minutes into the ascent, a large flock of Canada geese collided with the plane and disabled both engines. Engine power was lost, and in moments, Captain Chesley "Sully" Sullenberger also lost communication with air-traffic control. What to do? Relying on experience, the ability to stay calm under pressure, and a stunning display of creativity and chutzpah, he glided the aircraft eight miles and ditched safely in the Hudson River. All 150 passengers and 5 crew members survived.

When the downed plane began to take on water, several men tried to help the women and children evacuate first. Others pushed or jumped over their fellow passengers, desperately trying to escape. And a few blocked the way in an attempt to save their luggage . . . go figure. (They must have been lost in a good novel during that safety briefing that tells you to leave your stuff behind—yes, some people actually need to be told—in case of an emergency landing.)

Miraculously, all 155 souls got out. The last to leave was the captain, who walked the cabin twice searching for anyone who might have been left behind. The air temperature outside was a chilly 20 degrees Fahrenheit, but Sully and the crew peeled off their own jackets and gave them to freezing passengers as they awaited rescue.

Passenger Barry Leonard had jumped into the water before climbing into a raft and was soaking wet and in danger of succumbing to hypothermia. When the ordeal was over, he told a reporter, "I was obviously very cold and one of the crew turned to me and said, 'Please take off your wet shirt and I'll give you my dry one.' And he gave me his shirt. He literally gave me the shirt off his back to keep me warmer. I still have it. And I'm never going to give it up."[1]

Reversing the Flow

Reversing the flow is a term I learned from Susan Baggett and Thomas White, who run a yearlong course in service at the Center for Purposeful Living in Winston-Salem, North Carolina. Reversing the flow takes the spotlight off self-concerned "I, me, and mine" thinking and puts the focus on someone else's needs instead. The result of this compassion is that both the giver and the receiver feel better. When passenger Barry Leonard told the reporter that he wasn't ever going to give up that crew member's shirt, he said it all. Moments of compassion and generosity are worth preserving and reliving in our imagination. The positive emotions they evoke are deeply spiritual and expansive. They remind us of what it means to be fully human.

His Holiness the Dalai Lama has another term for reversing the flow. He calls it being *wise selfish,* since it's a smart way to serve yourself while helping others. Research on the health benefits of altruism bears him out: giving to others reduces stress, boosts well-being, offers meaning and purpose to life, and even helps you live longer.

Experiencing Flow Reversal

During my tenure as a cancer cell biologist, I finally hit the career wall. Worried that a grant I'd written wasn't going to get funded and that my research program would go belly-up, all I could think about was myself. Since Harvard had a "publish or perish" policy, not getting a grant might mean not having a job. For weeks I walked around tense, irritable, and all wrapped up in myself. It wasn't a pretty sight. Then one day my beeper went off at the clinic. An AIDS patient had requested a "peace of mind consult." No one had ever heard of such a thing, but because I was a meditation teacher, I was called to this man's bedside.

I went to "Sam's" room gowned, gloved, and if the truth be known, trembling inside. The virus hadn't been isolated yet, and I wondered whether I was putting my family in danger of contagion. Then, of course, there was another big question: how could anxious me facilitate someone else's search for peace? I pulled up a chair and we talked about life as dusk began to fall and the setting sun flooded the lonely room with delicate pink light. I taught Sam how to meditate and then held his hand for a few minutes until he fell asleep. Although he was close to my own age, he looked younger and more vulnerable.

He is some mother's child, I thought, *and right now, I'm the only mother on duty.* Watching his haggard features relax, my own troubles started to fade. Caring for him had reversed the flow of attention from my own worries to concern for a frightened and sick human being. Because of Sam, helping AIDS patients became my vocation in the early years of the epidemic, before effective drug cocktails rendered it a chronic illness rather than an immediate death sentence. While I still enjoyed research, it took a backseat to helping the confused and traumatized young men who made up the first wave of AIDS patients. Setting up a clinic for them was wise-selfish. They taught me more than I can ever acknowledge and changed the course of my life.

An Experiment in Reversing the Flow

Now that you've read my story, it's time to experiment with one of your own. This will take 10 to 15 minutes, and it's really worth doing. It helps to have pen and paper handy, since I'll be asking you to recall a memory of compassion and answer some questions about it.

The deed can be recent or very old, and it can be as large as sitting with a person who's dying or as small as smiling at someone who's having a bad day. The only requirement is that it's authentic and deeply felt—that is, you performed the act with an open heart rather than in an offhand way.

For example, maybe you stopped on a street corner, dug around in your pocket or purse, and gave a few dollars to a person down on his or her luck. Something about the individual spoke to you—some conscious or unconscious connection called you to stop and perform this small act of kindness. Perhaps you shared a few words and left feeling touched in some way.

Recalling an Agape Moment

You might want to have someone read the following instructions to you for recalling an *agape* [uh-GOPP-ay] *moment* (an experience of compassion), or you can read them into a recording device yourself and then play them back.

1. Close your eyes and take a minute to settle down and relax. A simple way to do so is to pay attention to your breathing without trying to change it. You might notice that the breath feels cool when it enters your nostrils and warm as it leaves. Alternatively, you might notice that your belly swells when you breathe in and flattens when you breathe out. Try this for five to ten breaths. It's a simple and powerful way to calm your mind and body at any time.

2. Now bring your attention to the center of your chest. Imagine that you can breathe the air around you into your heart. Feel the air massage and soften your heart, and then breathe that soft feeling back out into the room.

3. Now recall a time when you helped someone and felt a compassionate connection. Bring the scene to mind. Where were you? What did the person look like? What happened between you?

4. Now let the memory go and be mindful of the feelings left in your body.

5. Open your eyes and write down a list of what you're feeling.

THE POSITIVE EMOTIONS OF AWE, LOVE, JOY, FAITH/TRUST, PEACE, HOPE, FORGIVENESS, GRATITUDE, AND COMPASSION ARE SPIRITUAL IN NATURE BECAUSE THEY ARE EXPANSIVE AND WELCOMING. THEY RELAX YOUR MUSCLES AND BODY, ENABLING ENERGY TO MOVE FREELY. NEGATIVE EMOTIONS SUCH AS ANXIETY, DEPRESSION, AND ANGER CREATE TENSION AND CONSTRICT THE FLOW OF ENERGY.

What kinds of emotions did you experience when you recalled an *agape* moment? Do you have the list handy? Harvard psychiatrist George Vaillant considers the positive emotions of awe, love, joy, faith/trust, peace, hope, forgiveness, gratitude, and compassion as spiritual in nature because they connect you to life and expand your circle of concern beyond yourself. Vaillant writes:

———◆———

CHAPTER FOUR

Letting Go and Moving On

*"The moment you accept what troubles
you've been given, the door opens."*
— Rumi

When I was young, I moved in with a guy named "Jack" who gave my mother goose bumps—the kind that comes when your intuition screams trouble. After the frog-into-prince hormones wore off, I began to see her point about him. When our ill-fated relationship was finally dead and buried, I was free to move out and move on, which I did. But my mind stayed resolutely mired in the toxic territory of regret.

I couldn't open the door to the future because I was stuck in the past. *Why did I stay with that jerk for so long and let him take advantage of me? My life could have been so much better!* While authentic inquiry is important so that you don't repeat the same mistakes again, I wasn't asking the question in the spirit of inquiry. It was an angry and regretful activity, an obsessive rhetorical question anchored in the wish that I'd been smarter and made different choices. But I wasn't and I didn't. Those were the simple facts I needed to come to terms with; otherwise, I'd remain Jack's prisoner for life, subject to endless mental reruns of a movie that wasn't that entertaining to begin with.

In this chapter, we'll focus on moving on and letting go of regrets, grudges, and the frustrating habit of replaying the past and wishing that it were different.

Quit Arguing with Reality

Here's a bare-bones fact of life: *If you argue with reality, you will always lose.* Circumstances can't be any different from the way they are by definition; the conditions leading up to them are history. The chain of events culminating in the *now* happened in the *past,* and the past is over, so you might as well pay attention to what you've learned and focus on sharpening your skills to create a better future. Trying to change the past is pointless . . . unless you have the starring role in a science-fiction film.

When I finally accepted the Great Jack Fiasco and found positive meaning in it, I snapped back to my better self and came alive again. That, of course, is the basic definition of resilience—bouncing back when you hit the wall. I learned to appreciate Jack (once he was gone) as a masterful life coach who spared no effort in teaching me how to maintain good boundaries and stay true to myself. With that deeper understanding, it was possible to let go of what I'd done and celebrate whom I'd become as a result of our time together. The hard-won lessons of that less-than-stellar relationship opened the door to wiser and more loving ones in the future.

ARE YOU READY TO MOVE ON? IT'S TIME TO
ACCEPT YOUR LIFE AND MAKE PEACE WITH
THE PAST. ARGUING WITH REALITY WILL ONLY
STRESS YOU OUT AND WEAR YOU DOWN. SO
PICK YOURSELF UP, BRUSH YOURSELF OFF, AND
FIND POSITIVE MEANING IN YOUR EXPERIENCE.
ACCEPTING WHAT IS AND LEARNING FROM IT
IS THE FIRST STEP TOWARD A BETTER FUTURE.

Acceptance Isn't Wimping Out

Accepting the circumstances of your life is sometimes misunderstood as wimping out, knuckling under, or giving up—but, in fact, it's just the opposite. Accepting your circumstances realistically is the foundation for making positive, healthy changes. For example, the abused woman who accepts that she's in a dangerous situation ("I'm living with a violent man, and sooner or later I'm going to be hurt badly") is more likely to get out and get help than a woman who lives in denial ("He's not such a bad guy; he's just stressed out . . . if I do everything I can to make him feel good, then he'll treat me right"). Accepting reality means buying a one-way ticket out of la-la land.

Leaving fantasy and denial behind isn't easy since it means entering the unknown, but there's a lot to learn that only becomes obvious when you move out of your comfort zone. Staying in bad situations (how paradoxical that they're our *comfort* zones) seems preferable to moving on if you believe that the devil you know is better than the devil you don't know. That may be true if you're a sleepwalker who repeats the same behaviors over and over while expecting

Negative emotions are "all about me." In contrast, positive emotions free the self from the self. We feel the emotions of both vengeance and forgiveness deeply, but the long-term results of these two emotions are very different. Negative emotions are often crucial for survival—but only in time present. The positive emotions are more expansive and help us to broaden and build. They help us to survive in time future.[2]

HOW BIG IS YOUR CIRCLE OF COMPASSION?
DOES IT EXPAND BEYOND YOUR OWN CON-
CERNS, BEYOND YOUR IMMEDIATE FAMILY,
AND BEYOND THOSE WHO LOOK AND THINK
LIKE YOU? WHEN YOUR HEART EXPANDS TO
INCLUDE ALL LIVING BEINGS AND THE EARTH
ITSELF, YOU'LL FIND TRUE HAPPINESS.

The positive emotions that generate compassion represent a common spiritual ground available to everyone regardless of belief system. Virtually all religions agree that caring for others is inseparable from one's spiritual life. The behavior that leads to this goal in Christianity is called the Golden Rule: *Do unto others as you would have them do unto you.* In the Jewish tradition, it's stated this way: *What is hateful to you, do not to your fellow man. This is the law: all the rest is commentary.* The Japanese Shinto tradition expresses the same sentiment poetically: *The heart of the person before you is a mirror. See there your own form.*[3]

The Most Potent Force on the Planet

"Giving is the most potent force on the planet . . . and will protect you your whole life," says Dr. Stephen G. Post, director of the Center for Medical Humanities, Compassionate Care, and Bioethics at Stony Brook University in New York. Post is also president of The Institute for Research on Unlimited Love (IRUL), an Ohio-based nonprofit that has sponsored more than 50 studies by scientists from 54 major universities. The results are summarized in *Why Good Things Happen to Good People,* a book that Post co-wrote with journalist Jill Neimark.

Compassion improves the quality of life for both young people and adults. Teens who participate in community service are less likely to be depressed and have a lower rate of suicide than their less-generous counterparts. Furthermore, learning to help others tips the balance toward good mental and physical different results. But if you face your situation squarely and get the help you need to heal your past, then the devil will do a disappearing act.

Letting Go of Grudges

There's an old saying that holding on to a grudge is like swallowing poison to kill a rat. Unfortunately, the rat is spared while you suffer. Many abused women tell their therapists that the anxiety, depression, post-traumatic stress, and anger that remain after abuse is a lasting legacy. But it doesn't have to be if they learn how to forgive.

In a 2006 study conducted by psychologists Gayle Reed and Robert Enright, under the auspices of the Forgiveness Research Program at the University of Wisconsin, female subjects were trained to look for positive benefits in an abusive situation they had left. By doing so, they experienced significantly less depression, anxiety, and symptoms of PTSD and more improvement in self-esteem, forgiveness, environmental mastery, and finding meaning in their suffering than a second group whose participants were taught coping skills and given an assertiveness training program. The "benefit finding" women were able to clearly identify positive things they had learned and focus on them rather than on the familiar grievance stories that kept them miserable and stuck in the past.

"Holding on to anger is like grasping a hot coal with the intent of throwing it at someone else; you are the one who gets burned."
— **The Buddha**

Forgiveness Is for the Forgiver

The choice to let go of a grudge has nothing to do with condoning someone else's bad behavior. You can forgive a person while still testifying against him or her in court. Forgiveness is for the forgiver rather than the offender. It's all about taking your life back and moving on in peace, with a little more wisdom and compassion than you had before.

Psychologist Frederic Luskin, the former director of the Stanford University Forgiveness Project, wrote the important book *Forgive for Good,* which outlines nine steps to forgiveness that have been carefully researched. You can read about the specific steps on Dr. Luskin's Website (**www.learningtofor give.com**). His teachings involve commonsense principles that I've incorporated, added to, amended, and then boiled down to the following six steps:

The Six Steps to Forgiveness

1. *Get your story out.* Sift through your feelings about what happened, identify what you're not okay with, and tell someone you trust.

2. *Whatever hurt you is history.* The pain you're experiencing now comes from the bad feelings you're still carrying around—these are what forgiveness is meant to heal. When negative emotions take over, go for a brisk walk, try some belly breathing, meditate, make music, find something to laugh about, take

out your energy on a punching bag, or practice some other stress-management technique to help you change the mental channel.

3. *Living well is the best revenge.* Stop giving the person who hurt you the satisfaction of your misery—he or she has already taken enough. Learn to enjoy beauty, share friendship with good people, help others, have fun, and spread joy and kindness wherever possible.

4. *Life is not fair, so get over thinking that it should be.* Bad things happen to good people all the time. Your job isn't to even the scales of justice or punish anyone—including yourself. Your task is to enjoy life and help others do the same. If you make a habit of finding one new thing to be grateful for each day, you'll be happier and more motivated to change in constructive ways.

5. *Evict the victim.* Thinking of yourself as a victim may initially feel empowering, but it gets stale fast. Amend your grievance story to look for the hidden benefits that have made you wiser or stronger. Celebrate yourself as a *victor* rather than a *victim,* shut the door on the past, and move on.

6. *Be patient and vigilant.* Forgiveness doesn't happen overnight; it's a gradual process that can't be rushed. Be gentle with yourself when hurt feelings return periodically. Notice them, but don't marinate in them.

A NATIONAL SURVEY REVEALED THAT WHILE 94 PERCENT OF THE PUBLIC BELIEVES THAT FORGIVENESS IS A GOOD THING, ONLY 48 PERCENT HAVE ACTUALLY TRIED IT. HAVE YOU?

Change Your Grievance Story

Everyone has their own personal library filled with gripping grievance stories, and it's tempting to read and reread these dramas. After all, they're old friends. Here are some popular titles: *How Your Parents Ruined Your Life, The Boss from Hell, Scurrilous Wall Street Louses, Lost Loves and Other Betrayals,* and *Ungrateful Children.* One of Dr. Luskin's most sage pieces of advice is to turn those distressing stories into something to be grateful for.

Finding hidden positives is a common trait of resilient people. Dr. Dennis Charney, dean of Mount Sinai School of Medicine in New York, participated in a landmark study of 250 former POWS—many of them pilots who were shot down in Vietnam. Some suffered chronic stress and flashbacks that seriously affected the quality of their lives for years afterward. Others experienced far less depression and PTSD, despite an average of eight years of torture and solitary confinement.

Charney explained the difference this way: "Resilient POWs regarded their years in captivity as horrendous, but they learned valuable things about themselves that they would not have learned any other way, which prepared them to face challenges later in life." When you let go of your grudges and harvest your life lessons, you're ready to begin creating an optimal future.

In Part I, we explored the three secrets of resilience: a staunch acceptance of reality, a deep belief that life is meaningful, and the right-brain skill of improvising solutions. We investigated the explanatory styles associated with optimism and pessimism, learned how to dispute negative thinking, discovered the virtues of accepting reality, considered the benefits of compassion and spirituality, and learned to let go of past grievances so that we can look forward to and embrace new experiences.

In Part II, we'll delve into proven ways to retrain your brain—literally rewiring your nervous system in order to become more creative, compassionate, and resilient. That will prepare you for Part III so that you can, indeed, *become the future.*

Train Your Brain
for Success

◆

CHAPTER FIVE

Get Your Right
Brain Online

"Ashes to ashes
Dust to dust
Oil those brains
Before they rust."
— **Anonymous**

The average person generates between 25,000 and 50,000 thoughts each day.[1] I've always wondered how those clever researchers kept count, but it probably took a lot of planning, recording, and statistical analysis. The problem with all this thinking is that when stress sets in, the rational mind becomes less like a faithful servant and more like a firing squad. The majority of thoughts turn negative, which courts anxiety, anger, and depression.

You've already learned how to dispute your negative thoughts and think like an optimistic realist, but a lot of "thinking" doesn't come packaged in words. Images, physical sensations, dreams, and gut feelings provide vital information through the intuitive channel. This nonverbal way of knowing is processed, at least in part, through the pattern-recognition skills of the right hemisphere of the brain. Improvising your way to a better future (the resilient skill of *bricolage*) requires an active, flexible right brain to pick up subtle cues, make associations, and grasp the big picture. Then your left brain can fill in the details.

Daniel Pink, a best-selling author and journalist, wrote a book on retraining the brain to bring the right hemisphere up to speed. Called *A Whole New Mind: Why Right-Brainers Will Rule the Future,* his title is a play on words—the *whole* refers to using the entire brain . . . the right hemisphere as well as the left.

Pink's premise is that information used to be the currency that bought success, but with the advent of the Internet, acquiring a lot of data is less of a claim to fame than it once was. Information on just about anything—from nuclear physics to recipes for alligator fricassee—is a mere mouse click away.

The skill most needed for our postmodern times is *synthesis,* the combination of existing components into something completely new. Here's an example: Atoms of hydrogen and oxygen combine to create a molecule with emergent properties totally different from both atoms—H_2O. Water is wet and fluid, capable of transforming into ice or steam. It's a whole new creation. When we look at kids and wonder how they could possibly be so different from their parents, we're gazing at a miraculous synthesis, an emergent property greater than the sum of its parts. Our children come through us, but they are their own unique expressions of life.

Pink identifies the six right-brain aptitudes that facilitate synthesis and are needed in order to succeed in today's world. He calls these aptitudes the *six senses,* and the good news is that they can be developed. I'll give you a taste of each of them, but for more information, check out Pink's book *A Whole New Mind.*

1. **Design.** Why create a boring, boxy car just to get from here to there? For one thing, you'll go out of business. Energy-efficient technology is crucial in the

emerging world, but it's only part of what people are seeking. Aesthetic and emotional appeal slake the hunger for the beauty and harmony we long for as human beings.

2. **Story.** Ever go to a lecture and hear a great anecdote? You may forget the data that was presented in a day or two, but the story can inspire you for years. A good story stimulates imagination and is stored in the brain's limbic system where it can be evoked by emotions— rather than in the hippocampus, which encodes memory in language.

3. **Symphony.** By this, Pink means synthesis—intuiting the big picture that transcends the sum of its parts and births an emergent possibility.

4. **Empathy.** There's a big difference between scanning a résumé and under- standing the human being it represents. Emotional intelligence—which includes the capacity to feel and manage your

own emotions and those of others—
is a powerful predictor of success in
every sphere of life.

5. **Play.** Get those doctors at your hospital some finger paints. An art-therapist
   friend of mine did just that, and everyone felt better! Play creates spontaneity
   and facilitates synthesis, relationship,
   and positive emotions such as joy.
   Resilient people, by the way, laugh a
   lot. Playing games and enjoying light-
   hearted fun lubricate your brain as well
   as your relationships.

6. **Meaning.** In the developed world where
   getting and spending can deaden your
   appreciation of life's authentic pleasures, there's a voracious hunger for
   meaning and purpose that transcends
   commerce and greed.

In this chapter you'll explore brain-training activities ranging from humor to martial arts, mindfulness, yoga, and meditation. These activities will bring
your whole brain online and help heal your body,

mend your mind, refresh your spirit, and create brain circuits that favor resilient thinking.

Right Brain + Left Brain = Whole Brain

Since you have two brains (or more correctly, two hemispheres of the brain), resilience requires using both to your best advantage. When I was a budding medical scientist studying for my doctorate, I studied the work of the late Dr. Roger W. Sperry, a neuroscientist and professor at Caltech.

Sperry studied people whose corpus callosum (the thick tract of nerve fibers connecting the two hemispheres) was severed in order to treat severe epileptic seizures. Since no information could pass from one half of these individuals' brains to the other, the function of each hemisphere could be observed independently. Sperry won the 1981 Nobel Prize for these "split-brain" experiments, which yielded detailed information about the different functions of the two hemispheres.

The scientific dogma of Sperry's time was that the left hemisphere was more important than the

right. After all, it's responsible for language; deductive reasoning; and the kind of linear thought that lets you survey the fridge, make a grocery list, and drive to the market to get what you need. Its genius can send an astronaut to the moon or forecast economic trends over hundreds of years. (At least it used to be able to do that before economics became so nonlinear that logic, either the human or the computerized kind, is no longer enough to forecast the future.) The right brain, in contrast, was highly underrated. It doesn't "speak," and its mathematical skills are rudimentary (it can only add up to about 20).

But without the tasks that the right hemisphere performs, we lose much of what it means to be human—our creativity; our meaning-making apparatus; and the sense that we belong to a much larger, more mysterious, and more beautiful universe than logic can comprehend.

The right brain orients us in space and can read a map, but perhaps the most remarkable "map" it reads is the human face. Telling the difference between one face and another is a vital skill for living, as is reading the nuances of expression that reveal particular emotional states. Without this ability, we'd be like

Spock on *Star Trek*—devoid of the capacity to relate on a human level. And without right-brain function, we'd lose another critical aspect of humanity: our sense of humor.

Humor and Resilience

As I've discussed earlier, Drs. Dennis Charney and Steven Southwick interviewed former POWs, most of them pilots who had been shot down during the Vietnam War. Both doctors discovered that some of the subjects had a lower-than-average incidence of PTSD, and one of the traits that these resilient men all shared was a vibrant sense of humor.

For example, when John McCain, the senator from Arizona and former POW, ran for President in 2008, his legendary wit helped him discuss sensitive political topics with greater ease. It also humanized him and made him a hit on the comedy show *Saturday Night Live*.

Likewise, nurse/humorist Patty Wooten and psychologist Ed Dunkelblau wrote about how humor helped the entire country become more hopeful and resilient after 9/11:

> As professional comics returned to the stage and screen, they were careful and cautious. News headlines that appeared before September 11 suddenly became material for gags. Comics used opening lines like: "Well, I guess this sure takes the heat off the sharks." Or "Remember the good ole days of the West Nile virus?" Gradually comedians began to make jokes—not about the event, but rather about our nation's reaction to the event. One comic explained, "When President Bush said that we should resume consumer spending, I immediately went shopping. I mean, if I didn't, they'd be winning."[2]

A JOKE A DAY MAY NOT KEEP THE DOCTOR AWAY, BUT YOU'LL DEFINITELY FEEL BETTER. THE WEBSITE **WWW.AJOKEADAY.COM** HAS BEEN PROVIDING CLEAN LAUGHS SINCE 1995. HERE'S YOUR HOMEWORK: LOG ON TO THE SITE DAILY, PICK OUT A GOOD JOKE, AND TELL IT TO ANYONE WHO WILL LISTEN.

Drs. Shammi and Stuss, researchers from the University of Toronto, studied people who endured damage to the frontal lobes (located under the forehead) of their right hemispheres. Their findings showed that these individuals were less able to process humor, reacting to it by smiling and laughing fewer times than a control group. But even when a brain is "normal," some people are funnier and more appreciative of a good laugh than others.

As I've trained my right brain through years of meditation, yoga, and singing, I've definitely become more spontaneous, playful, and grateful for humor and comedy. The most spectacular humorist I know is my friend and colleague Loretta LaRoche, whom I call the Erma Bombeck of stress. Loretta has written and starred in several PBS specials and authored a number of smart, funny books with titles such as *Lighten Up!* and *Relax—You May Only Have a Few Minutes Left.* You can find out more about her work at: **www.Loretta Laroche.com.** I guarantee you'll feel better!

A HIGHLY DEVELOPED ABILITY TO IMPROVISE
AND SYNTHESIZE, FIND MEANING, FEEL
EMPATHY, LAUGH, AND PLAY ARE ALL RIGHT-
BRAIN ATTRIBUTES OF RESILIENCE.

Stepping to the Right of Your Left Hemisphere

Stepping out of your left hemisphere and into your right one creates resilience through multiple channels. It gives perspective through laughter, allows you to tune in to the needs and emotions of others whose love sustains you, instigates play, elicits the relaxation response by quieting down your thinking, encourages mindfulness, and sparks improvisation. Perhaps more important still, it connects you to a greater sense of meaning and purpose in life.

As a young neuroscientist, Dr. Jill Bolte Taylor had a massive stroke that temporarily disabled her left hemisphere, and in her words, enabled her to step to the right of it. The stunning experience of right-brain meaning and purpose that followed became the subject of her best-selling book, *My Stroke of Insight,* and a popular video that you can watch on the fascinating Website **www.TED.com**. (TED features a large number of short videos—each about 20 minutes long—of leading-edge thinkers sharing inspiring ideas for our times.)

When Dr. Bolte Taylor was a 37-year-old neuro-anatomist at Harvard, a blood vessel ruptured in the left side of her brain as she was getting ready for work one morning. Being a neuroscientist, she was able to observe what happened as her left hemisphere gradually shut down. During that time, she alternated between two realities—the distinct consciousness of each of the two hemispheres. In the right-brain state, she was euphoric, experiencing what she called nirvana (a sense of intimate relatedness to all that is and an ineffable feeling of deep peace and connection to a vast field of compassionate consciousness). Then her practical left brain would momentarily come back, and she'd realize that she needed help.

Getting that help was difficult, however, since the left hemisphere connects us to the external world, and Dr. Bolte Taylor was unable to speak or even walk. But eventually she was found and taken to the hospital. It took eight years for her to completely recover.

During an interview with Oprah, Dr. Bolte Taylor commented that she can return to that state of nirvana at will. We can all have this experience she suggests if we practice "running our right brain circuits of peace."

What you're about to read next is how your humble author, as a stressed-out graduate student in her 20s, learned to do just that through the practice of yoga and meditation.

Running Your Right-Brain Circuits of Peace

My personal interest in yoga and meditation began in the late 1960s. A grad student at Harvard Medical School, I was scared silly by the competition and began studying late into sleep-deprived nights. Migraine headaches, stomach pain, an immune disorder, chronic bronchitis, borderline high blood pressure, and anxiety qualified me as a bona fide wreck. In fact, some of my friends took to calling me "Psychosomatic Sally." Fortunately, one day in physiology lab, my partner "Jerry" taught me how to run my right-brain circuits of peace.

Looking up from a lobster claw that he was dissecting, Jerry commented that I had a very powerful mind. I was just beginning to bask in the praise when he added that my magnificent mind was also the hidden source of all my stress-related ills. *Well, that's an intriguing idea,* I thought, as I put down my scalpel to listen.

He said something like: "You create such vivid mental images that you mistake the movies of your mind for reality. Since your body can't tell the difference between what's actually happening and what you're imagining, it responds to your frightening fantasies as if they were real. You need to learn how to calm your mind and come back down to earth."

Jerry, as fortune would have it, had studied karate since he was a kid. All of the martial arts, he explained, are like meditation exercises that quiet your thinking mind and let your instinctual body wisdom take over. Then you can move organically and gracefully, picking up the slightest cues from your opponent on a nonverbal level.

Jerry was also a student of yoga, which, he assured me, trained the same kind of mental skills as karate. So I signed up for a yoga course. It was difficult at first, both because the postures (asanas) were new and because I thought success was becoming the perfect pretzel. It took several months to realize that the elderly woman next to me who could barely touch her knees, let alone her toes, was a great yogi. She knew that success is a matter of awareness, of paying exquisite attention to the feelings in your body and the movement of your breath—relaxing gently and mindfully into each pose. You can be a great yogi even if you're in a wheelchair.

I gradually learned how to relax and feel the underlying aliveness of the body. Once you feel that energy, you can understand what Dr. Bolte Taylor was describing about her stroke experience. When you access that field of energy that's within everything, no wonder you become aware of your opponents' energy in martial arts and "know" how they're going to move. In daily life, you become cognizant of people's moods—whether your boss is lying or telling the truth, whether a neighborhood is safe or dangerous, and other such right-brain skills known as intuition.

One day at the end of a yoga class, after I'd begun to feel some of these subtle shifts in attention and energy, I experienced an enlightening moment while I was in *savasana* (the corpse pose). I was filled with a deep, inexplicably wonderful sense of peace and thought, *Wow—this must be what people mean when they say relaxation.* This realization was an epiphany.

Relaxation tends to be a throwaway word used for kicking back. Take a bubble bath, get a massage, or go out to dinner and a movie. While kicking back does help to relax the muscles and mind, deep relaxation is a right-brain state of expanded awareness—a mindful immersion in the pleasures of the moment. Past and future become irrelevant since you're as firmly and flexibly anchored in the present as a sailboat rocking gently on its mooring. There's nothing to resist and nothing to desire. You're completely content and at home in yourself.

The Miracle of Mindfulness[3]

Most of the time, we're not home in ourselves at all . . . we're everywhere but here. A great meal often disappears efficiently without much appreciation of the subtle flavors and textures that the chef has so carefully synthesized. The moon crests over a hill and turns the landscape to milk and honey, but we may hardly notice the transcendent beauty. Our lover runs a gentle finger down our arm, but we're thinking of something else and the moment passes. This kind of mindless disconnection from life, so prevalent in modern times, causes stress in a species hardwired to connect.

Concentration meditation is simple in theory: You relax your body from head to toe, and then focus on your breathing. Every time you breathe out, you repeat a word or phrase that you've chosen. (Benson's original research utilized the word *one.*) When other thoughts enter your mind, the instruction is to simply disregard them. As Benson counsels, "Just say, 'Oh well,'" and return to the repetition of your chosen word as you breathe out.

For most people, the mind doesn't suddenly shut down and give up the ghost—its nature is to think. Meditation teacher Sogyal Rinpoche compares thought waves to ocean waves: whatever you do, the ocean will continue to rise up and make waves. In meditation, the goal is to "leave the risings in the risings" without catching the thought wave and riding it into the shore. Instead, just notice "thinking, thinking," then return to the repetition of your breath and focus word.

Meditation is like a mental martial art. As you gradually strengthen the muscles of awareness and letting go, you hone the capacity to choose your mental state. Instead of allowing the mind to control you, you learn to control the mind. Meditation makes it easier to disengage from obsessive and negative thinking throughout the day.

Although any word or phrase works for meditation, people with a religious orientation often find that using a short prayer provides added meaning to the practice and helps motivate them to do it. When I'm really stressed out, I like to repeat what may be the most popular prayer in the world: *Please God, help me!*

Since a lot of people enjoy guided meditations, I've produced several of them including *Meditations for Relaxation and Stress Reduction; Meditations for Self-Healing and Inner Power;* and *Stress Less: Meditations for Developing Resilience in Turbulent Times,* which is meant as a companion to this book. In addition, you might find my CD set *The Beginner's Guide to Meditation* helpful in inspiring your meditation practice. You can order these CDs from Hay House or **www .Amazon.com**, as well as from my Website, **www .joanborysenko.com**, where you can also sign up for a free newsletter, read articles, watch videos, and check on my teaching schedule.

CHAPTER SIX

Run Your Inner-Peace Circuits

"It seems we all agree that training the body through exercise, diet, and relaxation is a good idea, but why don't we think about training our mind?"
— **Sakyong Mipham**

When the economy began to sour and fear spread like a toxic fog through the country, Dr. Sanjay Gupta, chief health correspondent for CNN, encouraged stressed-out viewers to calm themselves with "compassion meditation."

Two studies published in 2008 alerted Dr. Gupta to the value of this ancient practice. One study, which was conducted at Emory University in Atlanta, assigned about 60 students between 17 and 19 years of age to either a meditation group or to a control group that held health discussions. The results were fascinating: Students in the meditation group who really did their homework (as opposed to those who meditated less frequently) were less reactive to stressful situations. They also experienced less inflammation in the body, which is important since inflammation is linked to depression and virtually all degenerative diseases including diabetes, heart disease, cancer, arthritis, Alzheimer's, osteoporosis, cognitive decline, and the frailty of aging.

The second study, conducted by neuroscientists Richard Davidson and Antoine Lutz at the University of Wisconsin, focused upon longtime practitioners of compassion meditation (16 Tibetan Buddhist monks) and 16 control subjects (who learned the meditation from scratch). Using functional magnetic resonance imaging (fMRI) of the brain in action, Dr. Davidson and his colleague found significant differences in the brains of the experienced meditators compared to the controls.

Compassion meditation decreases stress; increases the ability to empathize with others; and raises the happiness set point, which is a compelling finding because the beneficial feelings that result from satisfying external desires fade fast. (A few months after winning big lotteries, for example, people feel pretty much like they did before. And some are even more stressed because having a lot of money can complicate life . . . especially when others want to get their hands on it!)

Brain changes in the left prefrontal lobe of long-time meditators (most of whom live very simple lives) actually adjust the happiness set point to higher levels. It's a delight to be in the presence of such people because they're almost always smiling. They exude a kindness and contentment that's contagious, and are living proof that happiness comes from within. As long as a person has sufficient food, water, and shelter to meet the basic needs of life, research confirms that material possessions add relatively little to happiness.

Changes in the right-brain structures required for reading emotions on people's faces and sensing their feelings also occur in those who practice compassion meditation, which makes them more sensitive, intuitive, and emotionally intelligent. Emotional intelligence (EI)—the ability to identify, assess, and manage one's own emotions and those of others—is an active area of research in psychology, business, and education.

Popularized by psychologist and science writer Dr. Daniel Goleman in his best-selling book *Emotional Intelligence,* EI is highly correlated with success in all areas of life: leadership, management, parenting, teaching, creativity, friendship, and intimate partner relationships. Dr. Lutz commented that the capacity to cultivate compassion, which involves regulating thoughts and emotions, may also be useful for preventing depression in people who are susceptible to it.

Both studies of compassion meditation bring home the point that meditation only works if you do it consistently. So a strong commitment to practice on your part is necessary to make a difference in your brain state and health.

Here's how to start: read through the following script several times, pausing to experience the suggestions mindfully. Don't worry if you don't do it "perfectly." Just do what you can and use your heart intelligence to generate good wishes for yourself and others. When you finish the meditation, try reading through it again. After a few tries, you'll get the instructions down. Or if you prefer, you might read the script into a recording device and play it back for yourself.

Your Compassion Meditation Script

1.   Let your eyes close and allow yourself to be curious about what you're going to experience. Now roll your shoulders back, move your shoulder blades together, and let them slide down your back as if you were tucking a pair of wings behind you. This opens the chest and helps you breathe deeply and naturally. Rest your palms lightly on your uncrossed thighs, or cup them together comfortably in your lap as you relax your head, torso, and lower body.

2.   Bring your attention to your head. Imagine that you can breathe gently and easily into your brain. Allow your breathing to relax your eyes . . . your ears . . . the passages in your nose . . . your jaw . . . your tongue . . . your throat. Now imagine that you can breathe into the center of your chest. Let each breath massage and open your heart. Breathe that ease back out into the room. As the muscles of your chest "let go," feel

a wave of relaxation move through your shoulders and arms, hands and fingers. . . . Now imagine that you can breathe into your solar plexus, deep in your belly, where you sometimes feel sensations of inner strength and confidence—of natural mastery. Let that strength move like a stream of relaxed confidence down through your lower body . . . thighs . . . legs . . . and feet.

Return to your heart. Each breath in massages and relaxes the heart. Breathe that relaxation out into the room around you and extend the following good wishes silently, first to yourself and then to others:

- *May I be filled with loving-kindness.*
- *May I be well.*
- *May I be peaceful and at ease.*
- *May I be happy.*

3.   Now bring to mind one or more people whom you care about deeply. See them as clearly and in as much detail as possible. Breathe into your heart, and breathe out ease and kindness to them as you repeat these wishes:

- *May you be filled with loving-kindness.*
- *May you be well.*
- *May you be peaceful and at ease.*
- *May you be happy.*

4.   Bring to mind someone you feel out of tune with. Start off easy—think of an individual you care for and who cares for you. As your comfort with this form of meditation increases, you can pick more difficult people later. Breathe into your heart, and breathe out ease and kindness to whomever you've chosen as you repeat these wishes:

- *May you be filled with loving-kindness.*
- *May you be well.*
- *May you be peaceful and at ease.*
- *May you be happy.*

5.   Now bring to mind your country and her diversity of people: the poor and the rich, the healthy and the sick, the young and the old . . . individuals of all races, ethnicities, and religious backgrounds. Breathe into your heart, and breathe out ease and kindness to all of them as you repeat these wishes:

- *May we be filled with loving-kindness.*
- *May we be well.*
- *May we be peaceful and at ease.*
- *May we be happy.*

6.   Finally, visualize our planet as you'd see it from outer space—a beautiful blue and white orb spinning in the starry vastness. Imagine the vast oceans, snow-capped mountains, verdant plains, and expansive deserts. Bring to mind animals of every kind: those that fly, crawl, swim, and walk. Imagine people from every country, every tribe, every race, and every religion. Breathe into your heart, and breathe out ease and kindness to all as you repeat these wishes:

- *May we be filled with loving-kindness.*
- *May we be well.*
- *May we be peaceful and at ease.*
- *May we be happy.*

7.   Continue to breathe from your heart. With practice, compassion for all beings will remind you that you're part of a mystery much larger than yourself.

8.   When you're ready, come back and open your eyes. Continue sitting where you are until you feel ready to get up and go about your day refreshed with an open heart and mind.

Tips for a Successful Meditation Practice

1. *Choose the same place and time for your practice every day.* Try to reserve that place just for meditation. If you sit down in your TV chair, for example, you automatically shift out of everyday "doing" mode into a passive, receptive state. If you sit in your office chair, you go into work mode. If you sit in a meditation chair (or cushion on the floor), your nervous system becomes conditioned to run the right-brain peace program.

2. *Remember that it takes practice to learn meditation* —just like you have to practice in order to play a sport well or master a musical instrument. In the beginning, your attention is likely to wander and you may find yourself thinking a lot—that's normal. Just bring your focus back to the meditation, and pick up wherever you are over and over again.

3. *Give yourself a day off every week*, but do your best to practice consistently on the other six days. The more you meditate, the better the results.

4. *Let the people in your household know not to disturb you.* When my kids were young, we had a simple rule: meditation could only be disturbed for fire, blood, or other serious emergency.

5. *Know that pets enjoy meditative energy.* If your animal buddy can lie down and be quiet, that's fine. But if Fluffy or Fido wants to jump into your lap, keep your furry friend out of the room to minimize disturbance.

6. *Be patient.* Even if all you experience for the first several weeks is a wandering mind, you're still building the mental muscles of awareness and letting go of thoughts. Every time you catch yourself thinking or spacing out and then come back to the practice, you're wiring up new brain circuits that can help you release unproductive thinking during the day.

Meditating Informally

While learning to sit down and meditate is very important—and should be taught to every child in school—it can also be used more informally throughout the day. Dr. Benson used to tell the story of a busy Catholic priest who exercised, prayed, and meditated at the same time: when he jogged, he'd practice concentration meditation by repeating *Kyrie Eleison* ("Lord, have mercy") in time to the rhythm of his breathing and footsteps.

Mindfulness is also an exportable practice that makes everyday activities like eating more enjoyable. For example, Dr. Jon Kabat-Zinn teaches what he calls the "raisin exercise": Put a single raisin in your mouth and let it sit there for a while. Roll it around on your tongue—feel the texture and the saliva that's beginning to form. Bite the raisin so that you can taste the flavor, then chew it slowly for a long time, paying attention to the way your teeth, tongue, and throat cooperate to bring it into your body. Finally, notice what it feels like to swallow. The exercise might take five minutes or so, but it illustrates what it is to be truly mindful and aware of a process that's usually rushed and unconscious.

You might also enjoy *The Miracle of Mindfulness,* a short, practical book by Vietnamese monk and meditation teacher Thich Nhat Hanh. It's full of wonderful tips for bringing mindfulness into daily life while you eat, shower, do the dishes, and so forth. Mindfulness brings joy and pleasure to life. It's like pulling the plastic wrap off a piece of cake before you eat it—a much more satisfying experience!

Another way to make life more satisfying is to shift some of your attention off yourself and your concerns by moving your body, which changes the state of your brain very quickly and effectively. Exercise is a miracle drug that causes new brain cells to develop, elevates mood, and enhances stress hardiness and resilience as you'll discover in the next chapter.

✦ ✦ ✦

―――◆―――

CHAPTER SEVEN

Grow a Bigger Brain

"Too many people confine their exercise to jumping to conclusions, running up bills, stretching the truth, bending over backward, lying down on the job, sidestepping responsibility, and pushing their luck."
— Unknown

One of my favorite cartoons features a squirrel lying on a psychiatrist's couch, and the squirrel says something like, "Since discovering that you are what you eat, I realized I was nuts." When you recognize that despite all of your mental refinement you're still an animal engineered to move, it becomes obvious that lying around can also make you nuts. Brain chemistry goes south when you can't work off stress, and your mood becomes more negative . . . hostile, depressed, or anxious. The most effective way of improving your mind-set and enhancing the skills you've already learned is to simply get off your butt.

GET WITH THE PROGRAM! REGULAR AERO-
BIC EXERCISE ENSURES THAT YOUR BRAIN
CONTINUES TO PRODUCE NEW NEURONS AND
ADAPT TO CHANGE. DO YOU GET AT LEAST FIVE
HALF-HOUR PERIODS OF MODERATE EXERCISE
EACH WEEK? IF NOT, WHAT'S YOUR EXCUSE?

We all know that exercise is a good idea. It increases one's life span significantly since it reduces heart disease, cancer, osteoporosis, and a variety of other diseases, as well as increasing metabolism and regulating weight. In this chapter, we'll take a look at how exercise affects our brain and mood state. Regular aerobic exercise enables the brain to continue to grow and adapt to change by producing new neurons and rewiring its circuits throughout life.

"Rewiring" is an example of physical resilience, which enables the mental resilience dependent on it to function. After we check out some fascinating research, we'll take a look at why so few people actually manage to get moving and keep moving. And once we understand the most common blocks

to exercise, it's easier to overcome them and make a commitment to leading a healthy, active lifestyle. By doing so, we can then realize the incredible physical and mental benefits that await us.

This Old Brain Remodels Itself

When I was a student at Harvard Medical School, the dogma was that we were born with all the neurons we were ever going to have. We lose some as we age, but producing new ones just didn't happen. However, we know better now. More advanced methods of brain imaging have revealed that new neurons are created all the time as old ones die off. In this way, brain architecture changes and adapts to current circumstances, a form of remodeling called *neuroplasticity*. The new circuits have the power to transform the way we perceive the world, how we think, and how we act. They're the physical hardware that allows us to run the software (the thinking programs) we discussed in the first six chapters of this book.

Without moderate exercise, the brain not only fails to grow and remodel, but it can also shrink. Stress in particular causes the loss of cells and shrinkage of brain mass in areas critical for memory and planning. The U.S. Department of Health and Human Services recommends at least 30 minutes of moderate activity (such as brisk walking) five days a week, or 20 minutes of vigorous activity (such as running) three days a week. And this small investment of time has a spectacular payoff: it prevents the decrease in brain volume that begins in our 40s, optimizes brain function, blocks a lot of the cognitive decline (that is, fuzzy thinking and poor memory) accompanying aging and stress, and helps to lift depression.

Exercise Helps Trump Depression

Depression is a growing scourge in the United States. It affects 16 percent of the population and is estimated to cost about $83 billion a year in treatment and lost wages. And that doesn't even begin to factor in the cost of human suffering, which—if you or a loved one has ever been clinically depressed—you know all too well.

Depression can stop you in your tracks, sapping the will to live by initiating brain changes that lead to pessimistic thinking. That mind-set, in turn, creates

I've often wondered why we continue to sit on our butts even though we know so much about the benefits of staying active. And after years of encouragement by numerous health agencies and fitness magazines, between one-half and two-thirds of us still don't get even the minimum exercise necessary to maintain optimal health.

But now that you know what it does for your brain, you may be encouraged to stick with a consistent routine. You might also enjoy the story of how *I* got moving. And if you're not exercising regularly already, perhaps my experience may offer you the inspiration to start.

Couch Potato No More

When my kids were small, we lived in a rural area where the homes were spaced far apart. One day a neighbor banged on the door with news that the family down the road had just put out a kitchen fire. They had called her to mobilize help for the cleanup.

Since it was winter in New England, I threw on a coat and rushed out the door after my neighbor, who'd taken off at a steady jog. I tried to follow, but after a minute or two I was out of breath and puffing like a steam engine. Although I was just 30 years old, I felt ancient. Hunched over in the middle of the street with my hands on my thighs and gasping for breath, I had a come-to-Jesus moment. I realized that it was time to pay attention to my body, which, after all, was my only home.

That very night there was a show on public television about a woman in her 50s who had started to run a few years before and now jogged up to eight miles a day. Her transformation began by running to her mailbox and back, a distance of about a hundred yards. That didn't seem so hard—I figured if she could do it, so could I.

The next morning my three-year-old son, Andrei, and I set out together and took off at a steady clip. A minute later, I was bushed and slowed down to a walk, while he continued to jog along unfazed. It was a tad demoralizing to be outdone by a three-year-old, but I figured he had a lot less bulk to move so I persisted. Jog and walk. Jog and walk. Thinking of the PBS lady, I added an impromptu mantra to the regime. Breathing in, I'd think, *If she can do it,* and breathing out, I'd think, *so can I.* Soon I was like the little engine that could.

By the end of a few months, I was jogging three miles on most weekdays and five or more on the weekends. I lost a whole dress size, and along with it, some of my cravings for fatty foods. That's interesting in terms of body wisdom, since high-fat diets decrease the levels of BDNF (the hormone that stimulates new brain cells to develop). Jogging *increases* those levels, which is part of the reason why it grows your brain.

So what's a body to do when the food it's being fed produces a different result from the exercise it's being given? My personal experience is that the body adapts, and without much effort, your tastes begin to change. I began to eat more fruits and vegetables and less fat without even thinking about it.

Although there's a lot known about nutrition and mood, it's beyond our scope to go into that research here, but a good rule of thumb nutritionally is that what's good for the heart is also good for the brain. If you eat fresh, organic foods; limit fat and sugar; avoid processed foods; and consume at least five servings of fruit and vegetables a day, you'll feel much better and become a healthier person as well.

What's Your Excuse for Being a Couch Potato?

The top five reasons why people don't exercise are:

1. It takes time and most of us are already maxed out.

2. It doesn't necessarily feel great in the beginning.

3. Setting goals that are too ambitious can lead to giving up.

4. Giving to ourselves instead of others may feel selfish.

5. Name your own favorite rationalization. For example: It's too hot, too cold, too expensive to join a gym, too hilly to ride a bike, your elderly dog who can

hardly stand up whines if you go out
without her, you might miss an important phone call, your kids need a ride
to soccer practice, you don't have the
right gear, your spouse won't join you,
the baby has to nap, you have a test to
study for, it's too windy, the mosquitoes
are out, you're too fat to fit into
your sweats . . .

A fitness program takes discipline and continued
commitment before it starts to feel as comforting
as bad habits like eating junk food, smoking ciga-
rettes, drinking alcohol, or anything else that provides instant gratification but bites you in the back-
side later. If you keep at it, exercise is habit-forming
because the feelings of strength and well-being that
result are hard to beat. If you think you're ready to
take the plunge into a more enjoyable, less stressful
life (and yes—if there's any doubt about whether
you're healthy enough to exercise, get your doctor's
approval first), here are a few suggestions to make
exercise work for you:

— **Choose something fun and easy to get to.**
Personally, I'd rather be chased by a lion than go

to the gym. Gyms involve work. People have trainers and the whole thing seems like another job—with grades. My husband, on the other hand, *loves* the gym. He can gauge his progress and watch the news while using the elliptical trainer. And he almost always meets friends there—it's like a community center. I'd rather hike with our dogs, go for a bike ride, or cross-country ski in season. These activities start at the front door, which saves time and makes it much more likely that I'll do them.

— **Make exercise a nonnegotiable priority.** Putting yourself first means that you write exercise into a specific time slot on your schedule and treat it as an important appointment.

— **Exercise with a buddy, whether human or four-legged.** If someone is waiting, you're more likely to show up. Furthermore, social support is a proven stress reliever, so exercising with a friend does double duty for your health. The likeliest people to keep their exercise appointments, however, are dog owners. Dog walking more than doubles the average person's weekly minutes of exercise. The additional walking time burns off an average of 600 calories a week, which adds up to ten pounds a year in weight loss or weight that you don't put on.

In this chapter you've had a look at how even moderate exercise like brisk walking reduces stress, grows your brain, and helps ease depression. You've also examined how you can identify and overcome some of the excuses that keep you from doing it. All that lies between you and a better life is putting what you've learned into practice.

In the next chapter, we'll consider how the newly resilient you can find vision and purpose to become the positive future that our world needs now.

PART III

Become the Future

CHAPTER EIGHT

Living with Vision
and Purpose

*"The Constitution only guarantees the American
people the right to pursue happiness.
You have to catch it yourself."*
— Benjamin Franklin

Ben is a wiry, sandy-haired young man in his
early 30s. He likes to go rock climbing and mountain
biking, and is a committed environmentalist and
volunteer paramedic. His wife, Amy, is also an athlete
with a strong concern for the environment and for
the health and education of their two children. She
homeschools four-year-old Brett and his six-year-old
sister, Dawn. The family isn't wealthy, but they manage to pay their bills and enjoy a rich, loving home
life and lots of time outdoors in the magnificent
Pacific Northwest.

Supporting his family by doing something beneficial for others and balancing that with a busy home life is what Ben is all about. He's been the development director (fund-raiser) for a small nonprofit health clinic for four years, but when the economic downturn began, he became concerned that donations to nonprofits would decline, which they have. An optimistic realist, he could see that the river was turning, and unless he changed his course, he was likely to end up on dry land.[1]

Ben focused forward and began thinking about a new profession that he'd really enjoy—one that was recession-proof and in line with his values. Being a health-care provider struck him as a good bet, since it wouldn't be going out of style anytime soon. He loves the excitement of responding to emergencies as a paramedic and knows the ins and outs of the health-care system firsthand, so he decided to become a physician's assistant (PA), which requires credits in organic chemistry and biology before he can apply to a program. Ben still has his job as a fund-raiser for the time being, but he's already started taking the prerequisites for the PA program. Rather than thinking of the future as something that will happen to him, Ben is consciously creating it.

LIVE WITH VISION AND PURPOSE. RESIL-
IENT PEOPLE DON'T WAIT PASSIVELY FOR THE
FUTURE TO HAPPEN TO THEM—THEY BECOME
THE FUTURE BY CONSCIOUSLY CREATING IT.

The Present Is Pregnant with the Possible

Exploring your values and letting them guide your vision builds a bridge between where you are now and a future that can be even more rewarding than your past. The whole enterprise of envisioning what may come hinges on what my husband, Gordon, calls *double vision*—the capacity to see surface reality (and face it as Ben did) and the drive to explore the hidden treasures that lie beneath. Gordon loves to quote the late social psychologist Erich Fromm who said, "The present is pregnant with the possible."

Some of the questions you might think about if you're ready to develop the kind of x-ray vision that helps you see through the present situation to the possible future include the ones that Ben asked himself:

- *What do I value most?*

- *What are my greatest strengths?*

- *What skills that I already have can be most easily transferred to a new situation?*

- *What kind of new skills do I need, and how can I learn them?*

- *Who could advise me?*

- *What contacts do I have that might help?*

- *Is there a network of people with similar interests that I can join?*

You may want to reflect on these questions and then decide whether or not you're ready to take them further and create a values-driven mission and vision statement for your life. Times of change offer a natural opportunity to explore who you are, what makes you happy, and how you'd most like to live your life. If you're ready to devote some time to envisioning and manifesting your best future, the following section will help get you started.

Creating Your Best Future

The homework I'm suggesting will take several hours to complete, but the results are well worth the effort. While you can certainly do the process by yourself, it's particularly rewarding (and fun) to get a few trusted friends together for a day and do it as a small group. Sharing what each person discovers invariably deepens everyone's insights, strengthening the bonds of friendship and understanding. There are four parts to the process:

1. Think about what's most important to you. Take an hour or longer to write about your most cherished values. Here are some questions to guide you:

- At the end of your life, when you look back, what will mean the most to you? What do you want your legacy to be? Write an obituary for yourself that you'd feel proud of.

- What do you think the purpose of human life is? Do you believe you have a specific destiny? If so, are you on the right track? If not, how might you adjust your course?

• What do enjoy doing most? What are your strengths and talents?

• What are the weaknesses that get in your way?

• How do you want your loved ones— children, parents, and friends—to think of you?

• What kind of career is most appealing to you? The sky's the limit—if you want to be President but only have an eighth-grade education, that's okay. The assignment is to "blue-sky" about what you'd most like to do, rather than get bogged down in how you're going to get there.

• What do want to learn more about? Why?

2. **Ask your inner mentor for guidance.** We all have questions about life that we'd like to run past

a wise mentor, but sometimes we already know the answers. It's just a matter of retrieving them from the subconscious mind, which is connected to a greater source of wisdom than our own personal experiences. This process is one way to connect with that larger intelligence:

- Get into a relaxed state that favors reverie. You might play a musical instrument, meditate, do some yoga or stretching, or put on some relaxing music.

- Find a comfortable place to sit for about 20 minutes. Close your eyes and take ten deep breaths, imagining that you're going down one step of a staircase with each exhalation.

- At the bottom of the staircase, imagine going through a door and then following a path through beautiful woods to a sunlit clearing where there's a rustic wooden bench. Sit there. This is where your inner mentor will always meet you. Look around and find your mentor.

- Ask his or her name, and thank your mentor for coming.

- Ask any question that comes to mind. You might get an answer right away, or perhaps it will come later when you write about your experience in your journal.

- When you're finished, thank your mentor, walk back down the path, go through the door, and go back up the stairs to where you're sitting.

- Open your eyes and jot down your experience in your journal. The answers you're seeking sometimes become clearer as you write.

3. **Create a vision and a mission statement.** Now that you've spent some time contemplating your values and seeking guidance from your own wise self, it's time to write vision and mission statements that focus your intention. These clarify your goals and become the basis for creating step-by-step action plans to make your possible future a reality.

• A *vision statement* is the ideal life you want to manifest. It's the target you're taking aim at—the focus of your intention. Make sure your vision is detailed and covers all the important aspects of life, including love, work, purpose and meaning, emotions and feelings, spirituality, and finances. Here's my vision statement:

My goal in this lifetime is to become spontaneous and free, awakened, and compassionate so I can become the change I hope to see in this world. My career involves writing books and articles and speaking on topics of health, healing, and spirituality. I assist individuals and corporations in realizing their full potential. I value my loving relationships with my husband, children, grandchildren, and close friends; and I maintain a rich, sustaining spiritual life. I'm committed to cultivating optimal health and being in nature as much as possible. The creation of beauty and harmony is important in every sphere. I see a future that is financially independent and philanthropic, with an active and balanced work life that continues until my time on Earth is up.

• A *mission statement* is a precise and concise one-sentence description of what you or your organization actually does. It focuses your activities and helps you decide what opportunities are in line with your vision and goals. When employees understand their company's mission statement, for example, those firms have a 29 percent greater return.[2] The mission statement of my company, Mind-Body Health Sciences, LLC, is: *We synthesize information from the social sciences, biology, and the world's great wisdom traditions to inspire and assist individuals and corporations to create optimized lives and a more awake, compassionate world.*

4. Make a vision board. You may have heard about making a vision board, a collage that displays images of the future that you want to create. Can you find an image that represents your perfect soul mate? Your dream job? Your book on the bestseller list? (I wonder whose vision board that image is pasted on!) Going back to school? Birthing a child? Running a marathon? Comforting the homeless? Making peace in the Middle East? Touching God?

The process of creating your vision board is a form of bricolage. You're making the most creative collage out of whatever is at hand. Get a stack of old magazines, print images from the Internet, search through your photo collection . . . and your vision board will take on a life of its own. When it's finished, hang it in a prominent place where you can see it every day—that will keep your vision alive and your intention strong in the midst of a busy life.

Here are the supplies you need:

- A piece of sturdy white board at least two feet long and 18 inches high. (It can be even larger if you'd like. I prefer to use foam because it's easy to hang on the wall, and I also create smaller boards because they suit my office space better.)

- Old magazines, newspapers, photos, or other sources of images.

- Glue, scissors, and whatever other materials you like.

People who use vision boards often report stunning synchronicities. I know a woman, for example, who wanted to join the Peace Corps and volunteer in Africa, but after two years passed and she still hadn't been accepted despite much effort, she started to lose hope. However, about a month after creating a vision board, she got a call. She's now in Uganda, doing work with AIDS orphans. Is this a coincidence . . . or perhaps something more meaningful?

You are your own experiment. Make a vision board and see what happens. It's a positive step toward defining your goals and creating a conscious and fulfilling future.

✦ ✦ ✦

Just Do It!

"Discipline is remembering what you want."
— **David Campbell**

The world we once knew is in the process of dissolving and reforming . . . but it's not the end of the world. It's the beginning of a more just, compassionate, and cooperative era for our planet. Still, uncertainty is the order of the day, and we're in for a prolonged—and intense—period of change.

Here are ten brief reminders that will help you weather the transition and create a more positive outcome for yourself and for future generations.

1. *Give up trying to change the past*—it's history. Put 100 percent of your energy into creating a more skillful future.

2. *Mobilize resilient thinking.* Incorporate these methods into your life:

- Look reality in the eyes and accept what is.

- Find positive meaning in your situation.

- Use whatever is at your disposal to improvise solutions.

3. *Drop the victim mentality immediately.* Let go of grudges and regain your power.

4. *Exercise regularly.* Stress shrinks your brain, but you can reverse that trend by committing to a moderate fitness program. Be absolutely religious about this!

5. *Don't just sit there—do something.* Optimistic realists take action, but wishful thinking is a dead-end street.

6. *Don't just do something—sit there.*[1] Meditation reduces stress by eliciting the relaxation response, and it stimulates

the right-brain thinking necessary to
improvise your way to a better future.

7. *Stay engaged with life.* Alienation and
   isolation breed stress and depression.
   If you're depressed, get medical help
   immediately.

8. *Reverse the flow.* Helping others shifts
   the spotlight off your own troubles and
   releases feel-good hormones that heal,
   inspire, and give meaning to life.

9. *Think of one new thing at the end of each
   day to be grateful for.* Gratitude and other
   positive feelings enhance resiliency and
   help you become more expansive and
   compassionate.

10. *Connect with a friend.* Practice the teach-
    ings in this book with a friend so you
    can support each other as you enact
    positive, life-affirming changes.

ENDNOTES

Part I

1. This heading was inspired by the title of a book by psychologist Sonya Friedman, *Smart Cookies Don't Crumble: A Modern Woman's Guide to Living and Loving Her Own Life*. New York: Putnam, 1985.

Chapter One

1. Mickey Rourke, in response to a question by Jose G. Camil of Queretaro, Mexico, in "10 Questions," *Time* magazine, February 9, 2009.

2. T. H. Holmes and R. H. Rahe, "The Social Readjustment Rating Scale," *J Psychosom Res* 11(2): 213–8, 1967; R. H. Rahe and R. J. Arthur, "Life Change and Illness Studies: Past History and Future Directions," *J Human Stress* 4(1): 3–15, 1978.

3. "Facing Combat Without Stress? Researchers Examine Most Resilient Soldiers," by *Hartford Courant* staff writer Lisa Chedekel. It was published as a VA (Veterans Administration) News Flash on August 26, 2007, and can be located online at: **http://www.vawatchdog.org/07/nf07/nfAUG07/ nf082607-7.htm**.

4. Diane L. Coutu, "How Resilience Works," *Harvard Business Review,* May 2002.

5. Ibid.

6. George E. Vaillant, M.D., "Positive Emotions, Spirituality and the Practice of Psychiatry," *Mens Sana Monographs* 6(1): 48–62, 2008.

7. Ibid., pp. 48–62.

Chapter Two

1. Diane L. Coutu, "How Resilience Works," *Harvard Business Review,* May 2002.

2. The quote from Dr. Steven Southwick was taken from the article "Facing Combat Without Stress? Researchers Examine Most Resilient Soldiers," by *Hartford Courant* staff writer Lisa Chedekel. It was published as a VA (Veterans Administration) News Flash on August 26, 2007, and can be located online at: **http://www.vawatchdog.org/07/nf07/ nfAUG07/nf082607-7.htm**.

3. This introduction to the work of Salvatore Maddi on hardiness was adapted from a discussion by the American Psychological Association in their online series "Psychology Matters" in an article entitled "Turning Lemons into Lemonade: Hardiness Helps People Turn Stressful Circumstances

into Opportunities." It was published on December 22, 2003, and can be located online at: **http://www.psychology matters.org/hardiness.html**.

Chapter Three

1. David Williams, "Anatomy of a Miracle: How Captain Chesley Sullenberger's Skill Saved 155 Lives," *Mail Online*, January 17, 2009.

2. George E. Vaillant, M.D., "Positive Emotions, Spirituality and the Practice of Psychiatry," *Mens Sana Monographs* 6(1): 48–62, 2008.

3. The Shinto example is from an article on Beliefnet, one of the best sources for information on faith and spirituality: **www.beliefnet.com**.

Chapter Five

1. Hara Estroff Marano, "Depression Doing the Thinking: Take Action Right Now to Convert Negative to Positive Thinking," *Psychology Today* magazine, July/August 2001: **http://psychologytoday.com/articles/pto-20030807-000004.html**.

2. Patty Wooten and Ed Dunkelblau, "Tragedy, Laughter, and Survival," *Nursing Spectrum: Career Fitness Online,* October 22, 2001.

3. *The Miracle of Mindfulness* is the title of a book written by Vietnamese Buddhist monk and meditation teacher Thich Nhat Hanh. The complete reference for the paperback edition is: *The Miracle of Mindfulness.* Boston: Beacon Press, 1999.

Chapter Eight

1. Nina Zimbelman, a celebrated medical intuitive whom my husband, Gordon Dveirin, and I interviewed for our book *Your Soul's Compass,* also talked about giving up the fight with reality: "The more you accept what is," Nina counseled, "the more at peace you are. If the river turns, and you don't turn, you end up on dry land."

2. Watson Wyatt Work Study, cited by Susan M. Heathfield, "Strategy and Vision Statements," **About.com**: Human Resources, **http://humanresources.about.com/cs/ strategicplanning1/a/strategicplan.htm**.

Afterword

1. This was inspired by the title of a book by Sylvia Boorstein, *Don't Just Do Something, Sit There: A Mindfulness Retreat with Sylvia Boorstein.* New York: HarperCollins, 1996.

ACKNOWLEDGMENTS

The biggest challenge in writing this book was finding a title. I'm indebted to my friend, meditation teacher Sylvia Boorstein, for jumping up in the middle of lunch with a spirited "I've got it! *It's Not the End of the World!*"

Special thanks to friends and clients for sharing their lives and being such generous teachers. The stories and anecdotes about them are true to the spirit of the teaching, but none is literally true or modeled on any one person, living or dead. Most are composites that make the points I'm trying to illustrate without reference to any particular individual.

My husband, Gordon Dveirin, is my silent partner in this book. He read every word multiple times, made suggestions, and encouraged me shamelessly. The lively discussions we had are the connective tissue that gives this book form.

I'm so grateful to Karen Drucker for support, friendship, and her song "Loving Kindness" that inspired me to include a compassion meditation using her words. Chris and David Hibbard, Robin Casarjian, Kathleen Gilgannon, Luzie Mason, Debbie Ford, Cheryl Richardson, and Jonathan Ellerby . . . thanks to you all.

And to my Hay House family: Reid Tracy, your faith in me and the opportunity to keep writing are blessings that I never take for granted. Louise Hay, you are an inspiration to us all! Jill Kramer, thanks for being the good writing shepherd for the sixth time. Lisa Mitchell, thanks for your critical reading and suggestions. Thanks to Jenny Richards for the fine cover design. Margarete Nielsen, Sherry Wetherbee, and Heather Tate, you are angels for creating and maintaining my beautiful Website and newsletter. Richelle Zizian, New York Woman, many thanks for all the publicity. Many more of you at Hay House work behind the scenes in book design, customer service, and distribution. Please know how grateful I am for all that you do.

✦ ✦ ✦

ABOUT THE AUTHOR

Joan Borysenko, Ph.D., is a world-renowned expert in stress management and mind-body medicine. Her gracious presence, sense of humor, and ability to combine the latest scientific research with personal stories and riveting anecdotes make her a popular speaker in venues ranging from hospitals and corporations to conferences and retreat centers.

Joan received her doctoral and postdoctoral training at Harvard Medical School where she later served as an instructor in medicine. A biologist as well as a licensed psychologist and spiritual educator, she is a pioneer in psychoneuroimmunology and the cofounder and former director of one of the first mind-body clinics in the country.

Joan lives in a historic western town (population 170) in the front range of the Colorado Rockies with her husband, Gordon Dveirin, and their two canine companions, Sophie and Skye. A *New York Times* best-selling author who has written numerous books and produced a wide variety of audio and video programs—including the PBS pledge special *Inner Peace for Busy People*—she is also a journalist and the host of her own radio show. A former monthly columnist for *Prevention* magazine, Joan currently blogs in the Living section of the Huffington Post and writes for **www.Kashi.com**. Her work has been featured in numerous newspapers and magazines including *The Wall Street Journal, U.S. News & World Report, The Washington Post, O* magazine, and *Yoga Journal.* You can find out more about Joan, watch videos, and read articles at: **www.joanborysenko. com**. And be sure to visit her at **www.facebook.com** for live interaction.

NOTES

NOTES

NOTES

NOTES

NOTES

NOTES

NOTES

NOTES

NOTES

NOTES

NOTES

Hay House Titles of Related Interest

IF I CAN FORGIVE, SO CAN YOU:
My Autobiography of How I Overcame My Past and
Healed My Life, by Denise Linn

INNER WISDOM: Meditations for the Heart and Soul,
by Louise L. Hay

IT'S THE THOUGHT THAT COUNTS: Why Mind Over
Matter Really Works, by David R. Hamilton, Ph.D.

LIGHTEN UP! The Authentic and Fun Way to Lose Your
Weight and Your Worries, by Loretta LaRoche

All of the above are available at your local bookstore,
or may be ordered by contacting Hay House (see next page).

✧

We hope you enjoyed this Hay House book.
If you'd like to receive our online catalog featuring additional
information on Hay House books and products, or if you'd like
to find out more about the Hay Foundation, please contact:

Hay House, Inc.
P.O. Box 5100
Carlsbad, CA 92018-5100

(760) 431-7695 or **(800) 654-5126**
(760) 431-6948 (fax) or **(800) 650-5115** (fax)
www.hayhouse.com® • **www.hayfoundation.org**

Published and distributed in Australia by:
Hay House Australia Pty. Ltd., 18/36 Ralph St.,
Alexandria NSW 2015 • *Phone:* 612-9669-4299
Fax: 612-9669-4144 • www.hayhouse.com.au

Published and distributed in the United Kingdom by:
Hay House UK, Ltd., 292B Kensal Rd., London W10 5BE • *Phone:*
44-20-8962-1230 • *Fax:* 44-20-8962-1239 • www.hayhouse.co.uk

Published and distributed in the Republic of South Africa by:
Hay House SA (Pty), Ltd., P.O. Box 990, Witkoppen 2068 • *Phone/
Fax:* 27-11-467-8904 • info@hayhouse.co.za • www.hayhouse.co.za

Published in India by:
Hay House Publishers India, Muskaan Complex,
Plot No. 3, B-2, Vasant Kunj, New Delhi 110 070 • *Phone:*
91-11-4176-1620 • *Fax:* 91-11-4176-1630 • www.hayhouse.co.in

Distributed in Canada by: Raincoast,
9050 Shaughnessy St., Vancouver, B.C. V6P 6E5 •
Phone: (604) 323-7100 • *Fax:* (604) 323-2600 • www.raincoast.com

Take Your Soul on a Vacation

Visit **www.HealYourLife.com®** to regroup,
recharge, and reconnect with your own magnificence.
Featuring blogs, mind-body-spirit news, and life-changing
wisdom from Louise Hay and friends.

Visit **www.HealYourLife.com** today!

For a complete selection of Hay House products, visit: **www.HealYourLife.com®**

Yes, I'd like to receive:

- ☐ Information on the NEW Wisdom Community
- ☐ Information on the NEW Women's Wisdom Circle by Christiane Northrup, M.D.
- ☐ A Hay House Catalog
- ☐ The Louise Hay Premier Online Newsletter
- ☐ The Sylvia Browne Premier Online Newsletter

Name

Address

City _____ State _____ Zip _____

Phone

PLUS, if you give us your e-mail address, we will e-mail you a $10 coupon good for your online purchase at: **www.hayhouse.com**!

E-mail

To:

HAY HOUSE, INC.
P.O. Box 5100
Carlsbad, CA 92018-5100